INFORMAL READING INVENTORIES
Second Edition

Marjorie Seddon Johnson

Roy A. Kress
Professor Emeritus
Temple University

John J. Pikulski
University of Delaware

An **ira** Service Bulletin

Published by the
International Reading Association
800 Barksdale Road
Newark, Delaware 19714

Copyright 1987 by the
International Reading Association, Inc.

Library of Congress Cataloging in Publication Data

Johnson, Marjorie Seddon,
   Informal reading inventories.
   (Reading aids series) (IRA service bulletin)
   Bibliography: p.
   1. Reading – Ability testing. 2. Reading (Elementary)
I. Kress, Roy A. II. Pikulski, John J. III. Title.
IV. Series. V. Series: IRA service bulletin.
LB1050.46.J634   1987   372.4   86-18493
ISBN 0-87207-231-2

Cover by Boni Nash

DEDICATED TO
Marjorie Seddon Johnson
1918-1985

Marjorie Seddon Johnson died on December 31, 1985, as this book was in its final stages of preparation for publication. Coauthor of this and the first edition of *Informal Reading Invento-ries,* Marjorie's understanding of the reading process and of those who read is reflected throughout the volume, as it is in all of her writing about education. A master teacher, her stance in the classroom (in the secondary schools of Springfield Township, Pennsylvania, for nine years and then at Temple University for thirty-six years) will serve as a model for those of us who strive to *ed•u•cate* – to foster the growth and expansion of knowledge.

Author, scholar, teacher, humanitarian, colleague, friend, Marjorie was far ahead of the researchers and educators of today who strive to understand and foster thinking and reading comprehension. This educator sought no panaceas. To her, teaching was work, and she worked at it. If she was ever intolerant, it was of those who refused to apply their own cognitive skills to the solution of a problem. In response to a question voiced by a student in a graduate class, Marjorie's usual reply was, "What do *you* think?" And she certainly knew how to wait for a response! When none was forthcoming, she would begin to provide clues to possible answers, leading the student to a solution and often to alternative ones as well.

Perhaps the best representation of her contribution to the teaching profession is to be found in a recent statement by Carol Santa, one of her former graduate students: "She made such a significant impact on my life, as a role model for scholarship and love for other people." This sentiment is echoed by thousands of her students and, by the ripple effect of a fine teacher, by a legion of children everywhere! We do, and will continue to, miss her.

RAK
JJP

Contents

Foreword

More than twenty years ago, the first edition of *Informal Reading Inventories* was published by the International Reading Association. Distribution figures indicate that the Marjorie Seddon Johnson and Roy A. Kress monograph has been the organization's most popular publication. Thousands of teachers have learned and their students have benefitted from the comprehensive treatment of informal reading inventories presented in the first edition. John J. Pikulski joined the two original authors in preparing this revision. It seems most appropriate that this revised publication be dedicated to Professor Johnson, whose death occurred near the completion of the manuscript.

As the authors point out, the idea of informal reading inventories is not new. Even though such informal procedures can be traced back to the 1920s, there is still a great need for a publication like this one. Three highly competent professionals, who have spent much of their professional careers devoted to studying reading and reading evaluation, have integrated their knowledge about informal evaluation procedures into this revised monograph. New teachers—and experienced teachers who have not used IRIs—can learn much about IRIs from this publication. Teachers who already use IRIs also are likely to find suggestions to help them improve their use of such procedures.

In the hands of knowledgeable teachers, the approach described in this publication can furnish better diagnostic and evaluation data than can be obtained through use of standardized, norm referenced tests. Further, an IRI as outlined in this second edition of *Informal Reading Inventories* may use testing materials taken from pupil texts, thus making testing and teaching materials comparable. In a sense, books are tried out to see if they "fit" instruction or independent reading. The teacher observes strengths and weaknesses as students read both orally and silently.

The accuracy and usefulness of decisions made from IRI data depend heavily on the expertise of the examiner. Directions and descriptions of IRIs included in this publication are clear enough and complete enough to make it fairly easy for a teacher who studies them carefully to construct good inventories, to administer them efficiently, and to interpret the results accurately.

Like the original publication, this revision is highly practical and thorough. It has been updated on research and theory related to IRIs and has more detailed explanations of procedures. This second edition also compares IRIs with other approaches used in assessing reading achievement. Though the basic ideas of the original are retained, the earlier version has been almost completely rewritten.

As the first editor of the Reading Aids series, it was my privilege to edit the 1965 edition of *Informal Reading Inventories*. The fact that the original publication was the "best seller" among IRA publications for many years attests to the outstanding work of the coauthors in the first edition. I predict that this updated edition will continue the record breaking pace set by the first edition and will serve the International Reading Association well for another twenty plus years.

Ira E. Aaron
Professor Emeritus
University of Georgia

Preface

The purpose of this volume is to provide a comprehensive description of one approach to evaluating reading—the use of informal reading inventories (IRIs). Educational evaluation can serve many purposes. However, our goal in writing this volume is to provide teachers and reading specialists with practical strategies to help them form diagnostic impressions they can use in planning the advancement of reading proficiency in their students. In our opinion, evaluation procedures are of no value if they do not lead to improved instruction and improved student performance.

The evaluation of so complex a phenomenon as reading is a formidable task—one requiring professional knowledge and careful thought and analysis. We see informal reading inventories as a very useful approach to helping teachers or specialists develop a beginning understanding of how children approach the complex phenomenon called *reading* and how teachers might help such children become increasingly more masterful in the use of this important tool for communicating with other people. We maintain throughout this volume that the results of IRIs are not static, highly precise scores; instead, the results yield a set of working hypotheses or informed, professional opinions that are to be confirmed, denied, extended through continuous observations of children's behavior as they engage in the process of reading. The results of an evaluation using an IRI are not an end product, but a starting point for giving more informed answers to the question: "What should I as a teacher do to help these children become more proficient readers?"

To teach reading and to evaluate reading one must have in mind a clear concept of reading. Though current descriptions of the reading process are incomplete (and often contradict one another), we think it essential that all teachers who are engaged in teaching or testing reading develop their own concept or theory of what reading is, no matter how incomplete that concept or theory may be. A brief summary follows of the ideas we have about reading—ideas which serve as guides to much of what appears in this volume.

Reading: A Language/Communication Process

People, as social beings, are constantly involved in situations which demand efficient communication. Reading is simply one facet of the total communication process, though it assumes a vital importance as the individual matures and the amount of reading materials in the world proliferates.

Development of reading ability, however, does not take place in a vacuum apart from growth in other facets of communication. Listening, speaking, reading, and writing have certain common elements. Growth in one tends to be associated with growth in another and all build from a common base of experience, of knowledge of the world. The broader that experience/knowledge base, the greater the potential for communication. Most human beings develop listening and speaking skills without formal instruction. Reading and writing, though manifesting some spontaneous growth, are usually taught as part of the responsibility of the school. However, as facets of communication with many common elements, the listening and speaking skills that children bring with them to school form an essential part of the foundation for reading and writing skills. In addition, developing readers must learn the conventions of written language and how these relate to previously developed oral language skills. While the process called reading may be temporarily, artificially broken into skills which can be taught as aids to helping children master the total process, it is essential to bear in mind that the skills are not ends unto themselves. They are useful only if they contribute to the communication/thinking aspects of reading.

The purpose of this volume is not to try to articulate a theory of reading; however, it seemed important to point out that the authors see reading as a very small part of the complex process of communication. Given this complex view of reading, the goals of this volume are extremely modest. Clearly, it would be impossible, in one short volume designed to offer teachers and reading specialists practical suggestions for evaluating reading, to address all possible language/communication considerations.

MSJ
RAK
JJP

Chapter 1

The Purpose and Nature of Informal Reading Inventories

Introduction

The teacher of reading is constantly faced with a multitude of questions:

"Rob really seems to be having difficulty working in his present reading group. Should I move him to another group?"

"The information Mr. Norman gave me, based upon his work with this class last year, gives a good idea of how to group those children for instruction, but what do I do with the two new students in my class who just transferred to this school?"

"Jane does fine with some of the activities in her reading program, but at other times she seems to run into problems. How can I get a clearer picture of her strengths and weaknesses in reading?"

"Gary had a grade score of 4.3 on the standardized reading test he took last year, but he is clearly having trouble working in a fourth reader level book. What kind of testing can I do to further check my judgment that he should be moved to a different reading group?"

This list of questions could go on and on. There appears to be widespread agreement among teachers that reading instruction should be at an appropriate level of challenge for each student and should be planned on the basis of the strengths and needs the student has in reading. Most teachers are genuinely concerned about basing their reading instruction on valid information about the pupil's present level of achievement, and about the strengths and weaknesses the pupil brings to that instruction. Unfortunately, teachers frequently feel at a loss to obtain such diagnostic information.

A confused, almost chaotic picture often exists of the area of evaluating reading skills. The most recent *Tests in Print III* (Buros Institute of Mental Measurement, 1978) lists 267 tests of reading. How is the teacher to choose from such a vast array? What criteria should be used for choosing tests of reading ability? To make matters worse, it appears that many of these reading tests are of poor quality. Schell (1981) cites Oscar Buros, an outstanding test critic, as having indicated that at least half of the tests available never should have been published. Teachers and reading specialists feel overwhelmed by the large number and wide variety of tests that exist and with the expanding volume of technical information that accompanies these tests. It is not that teachers fail to recognize the need to evaluate a pupil's level of achievement; they frequently seem unable to employ the evaluation procedures needed to obtain such information. The purpose of this publication is to describe as completely as possible one major approach to the evaluation of reading performance—Informal Reading Inventories.

Informal reading tests are not new. In his historical overview of the development of IRIs, Beldin (1970) traces their use back to 1920. In a broad sense, IRIs can be thought of as structured observations of reading performance. The authors of this publication feel strongly that no reading test currently available, or likely to be available in the foreseeable future, can serve as a substitute for the careful, continuous observations a capable teacher can make as a child responds during reading instruction. This essential, day to day observation can supply the answer to almost all diagnostic questions teachers are likely to pose about a child's reading. However, since much reading instruction takes place in groups and carries with it the obligation to teach, not just to observe, it is often difficult for a teacher to obtain all of the diagnostic information needed. Informal reading inventories, therefore, enable teachers to focus all of their efforts on diagnosis and evaluation in a more structured way and on an individual's performance, even when the instrument used is a group IRI.

IRIs can take several different forms, but before exploring those forms, it might be best to point to the shared characteristics. To begin, consider the basic noun, *inventory.* An inventory deals with a comprehensive, detailed cataloging of items or traits. An IRI is a detailed study of an individual's overall performance in the area of reading as well as some of the language and thinking skills which are a necessary part of the reading process. In the term *informal reading inventory,* reading is seen as highly related to language and thinking. While IRIs allow for a thorough, careful evaluation of word identification skills and strategies, such skills are seen as serving the area of reading comprehension, which includes the understanding of the written messages intended by the author and the active manipulation of the ideas represented through print. The techniques recommended in this publication are informal, allowing flexibility in and adaptability of their use. The use of IRIs is aided by a series of guidelines for their construction, administration, scoring, and interpretation. However, use of these inventories is not bound by formal directions, defined time limits, or a restricted set of materials or procedures. Finally, the results of IRIs do not match an individual's performance against standardized or normed scores. Instead, the individual is evaluated against preestablished standards which must be met if that individual is to become a successful, accomplished reader of the materials ultimately determined appropriate for use in classroom instruction. The emphasis is not upon comparing the performance of someone who is taking an IRI with others who have taken such inventories; instead, the emphasis is on learning about the skills, abilities, and needs of the individual in order to plan a program of reading instruction that will allow a maximum rate of progress.

An IRI, therefore, offers the opportunity to evaluate children's actual reading performance as they deal with materials varying in difficulty. While an appraisal of specific reading skills and strategies is being made, opportunities also arise for making informal evaluations of other facets of communication.

Purposes of Informal Reading Inventories

No testing instrument can be evaluated except in relation to the purposes for which it is used. IRIs can satisfy a number of important and practical educational needs.

Estimate Reading Levels

Careful administration of an IRI can determine the level at which the child is ready to function independently in reading, the point at which the child can profit from teacher directed reading instruction, and the level where the child reaches complete frustration. It is important for a teacher to know the level of reading material the child can handle adequately when working alone. Most school work (certainly that reading which will make the student a mature and avid reader) is done on an independent basis. Unless materials are provided at the proper level, children cannot be expected to do an adequate job in independent work and establish for themselves high standards of performance, or experience the self-confidence which comes from the successful completion of an assigned or self-assumed task. Instructional work should be provided at a level where the child meets sufficient challenge to learn and yet can be expected to be reasonably successful if proper instruction is given. A child interacting with materials at an appropriate instructional level will meet challenges in either word identification or comprehension skills. As a result of that interaction, plus direct teacher guidance and instruction, the child will achieve full mastery of the material at the conclusion of the instruction. However, to give instruction in materials which the child can handle virtually independently would be wasteful of the limited amount of teacher time available for direct instruction.

Diagnose Strengths and Weaknesses

A second major purpose to be served by the IRI is the determination of the child's specific strengths and weaknesses. Only through careful analysis of specific skills and strategies and the pupil's adequacy of achievement of these skills can a suitable instructional program be planned. Teaching at the right level is not enough. Instruction must be directed toward overcoming any existing specific weaknesses. Instruction also must be given in areas where the child has adequate readiness for learning. For instance, a child may have difficulty in hearing as separate units the sounds which constitute a word. More specifically, the student may have difficulty dealing with the concept of the beginning sound in a word. This same child may have difficulty associating letters and the sounds they commonly represent. The first skill is more fundamental than the second. Until the child develops sufficient sensitivity to language to be able to hear the separate sounds that constitute a word (called auditory segmentation), instruction in letter sound associations as an aid to word identification seems unnecessary and probably doomed to failure.

Lead to Understanding the Nature of Reading Problems

Third, IRIs can help a teacher to understand more fully why a child is experiencing difficulty with some aspects of reading; that is, IRIs can lead to a fuller understanding of the nature of some reading difficulties. For example, to learn that a child is having difficulties with reading comprehension is limited in its implications for instruction. Does the comprehension problem seem largely reflective of inefficient word identification strategies, limited vocabulary development, weak experiential background, unwillingness to draw inferences because of a fear of being wrong, or some other reason? The administration of an IRI often can move an examiner toward a much clearer understanding of the probable source or sources of reading comprehension difficulties.

Help Bring Self-Understanding to Readers

A fourth purpose of the inventory is to help learners become more aware of their levels of achievement as well as specific strengths and weaknesses in reading. As readers work with materials of increasing difficulty, they should be able, with the aid of the teacher, to determine when the reading is going well and when assistance is needed. In the same fashion, an awareness can be developed of the kinds of thinking and word recognition they are capable of handling, and those in which improvement is needed. With increased learner awareness, instruction becomes more effective.

Evaluate Progress

A final purpose to be accomplished by an inventory is that of evaluation of progress. Repeated inventories at periodic intervals will make it possible to determine changes in level of reading achievement and in the development of more specific skills and strategies. In this way, a clearer measure of a child's growth can be obtained. Such information can be extremely valuable in communicating with fellow teachers, other professionals, and parents—all of whom are concerned with the progress of an individual child.

Among their major strengths, IRIs have great flexibility which, in many cases, is vital to accomplishing the purposes just discussed. However, with this flexibility comes the examiner's responsibility for making judgments; thus the extent to which the purposes are accomplished will depend on the competency of the examiner. Because the usefulness of the inventory depends on accurate observation of the individual's performance during the testing, and interpretations based on these observations, only a competent examiner can accomplish the purposes outlined.

Informal Reading Inventories Compared to Other Approaches to Evaluating Reading

To help build a better understanding of the nature of IRIs, their uses, their strengths and limitations, it will be helpful to review other major approaches to evaluating reading: standardized reading tests, miscue analysis, criterion referenced tests, and the cloze procedure.

Standardized Reading Tests

Basically, the score obtained from a standardized reading test allows comparisons: one can compare the performance of the person taking it to the performance of others who have already taken the test. The individual's test performance generally is expressed as a specific numerical value such as a grade equivalent score, a percentile rank, or a standard score. For example, if an individual achieves a percentile score of 65, it means that person answered more items correctly than did 65 percent of the group who took the test and to whom he or she is being compared. The student did better on the test than 65 percent of the other people in the group.

One widespread misuse of standardized test scores is interpreting a grade equivalent score from such tests as reflecting the grade level at which an individual should receive instruction. Grade equivalent scores were not meant to be interpreted in this way. The following is part of a resolution endorsed by the Delegates Assembly of the International Reading Association in April 1981.

WHEREAS, one of the most serious misuses of tests is the reliance on a grade equivalent as an indicator of absolute performance, when a grade equivalent should be interpreted as an indicator of a test taker's performance in relation to the performance of other test takers used to norm the test, and

WHEREAS, in reading education, the misuse of grade equivalents has led to such mistaken assumptions as: 1) a grade equivalent of 5.0, on a reading test means that the test taker will be able to read fifth grade material, and 2) a grade equivalent of 10.0 by a fourth grade student means that the student reads like a tenth grader even though the test may include only sixth grade material as its top level of difficulty....

RESOLVED, that the International Reading Association strongly advocates that those who administer standardized reading tests abandon the practice of using grade equivalents to report performance of either individuals or groups of test takers and be it further

RESOLVED, that the president or executive director of the Association write to test publishers urging them to eliminate grade equivalents from their tests.

Thus, the International Reading Association labels the drawing of conclusions about the level of material a pupil can read as a "misuse" of grade equivalent scores from standardized reading tests. In short, while grade equivalent scores may be useful in making some rough divisions among achieving and non-achieving readers, unless new evidence is forthcoming, standardized reading tests do not seem to be appropriate instruments for the reading instructional placement of individual students. IRIs are more suitable for this purpose.

Miscue Analysis

Miscue analysis has developed largely from the research of Kenneth and Yetta Goodman which focused on a comprehensive, detailed analysis of recordings of oral reading performances. "Miscue analysis involves its user in examining the observed behavior of oral readers as an interaction between language and thought, as a process of constructing meaning from a graphic display. The reader's use of graphic, phonological, syntactic, and semantic information is considered" (Goodman, 1973, p. 4). A miscue occurs when readers read something different from what is printed in the text they are reading. The term *miscue* is preferred over *error* by advocates of this approach since they maintain that error implies a randomness, whereas the reasons for the occurrence of most miscues can be inferred. Like IRIs, a major purpose of miscue analysis is to qualitatively analyze a reader's miscues in order to decide the reading strategies being used and the areas of strengths and weaknesses. In miscue analysis no attempt is made to establish reading levels based on the number or percentage of miscues made or on the number or percentage of comprehension questions answered.

Because of the emphasis upon qualitative interpretation for an individual's reading performance, an inaccurate contrast is often made with IRIs, which are erroneously said to rely only on calculation of accuracy scores. Nothing could be further from the truth. While experienced, capable users of IRIs use quantitative criteria as starting points for the establishment of reading levels, they definitely recognize the need to take into consideration the nature and quality of the errors made. In addition, users of IRIs analyze the nature of the individual's responses in order to determine the strategies being used by the reader and the skills and possible weaknesses involved. These aspects of IRI use will be developed throughout this publication. (For a more detailed discussion of miscue analysis see K. Goodman, 1973; Y. Goodman & C. Burke, 1972).

Criterion Referenced Tests

Criterion referenced tests in reading share a number of similarities with IRIs. Like IRIs, criterion referenced tests compare an individual's performance to an absolute, preestablished standard rather than to the performance of a group of individuals. The form most criterion referenced tests have taken, however, has made them very different from an IRI. In an IRI the attempt is to deal with reading as holistically as possible, in a form as close to "natural" reading as possible. Most criterion referenced tests have reflected attempts to break reading into many (sometimes hundreds) subskills and to judge adequacy of reading on the basis of performance on those separate subskills. Few, if any, have included natural text or sustained reading activities. Another problem with criterion referenced tests is that the criteria for judging the adequacy of an individual's performance have often been arbitrary. Most criterion referenced tests were designed for group use and most used a multiple choice format, unlike a test of real reading in which one must produce responses. While criterion referenced tests created great excitement and enjoyed great popularity from the mid sixties to the mid seventies, their use appears to be waning, perhaps because many were of highly suspect quality.

Cloze Procedure

In several respects, the cloze procedure is an informal procedure. It is not governed by a large number of restrictions regarding its construction and administration. The user of this procedure has great flexibility. It shares with IRIs the quality of having a close relationship to instructional materials. Like IRIs, cloze tests can be constructed from instructional materials a teacher is considering for use with students. Cloze can be used as a way of estimating a student's instructional level placement.

Cloze tests are very easy to construct. In their most frequently used form the first sentence of the reading materials is left intact; thereafter, every fifth word is deleted, usually until there are approximately fifty blanks. Cloze tests typically are administered in groups. The task of the student is to try to reproduce the words deleted.

As an informal approach to evaluating reading, the cloze procedure has much to recommend it: it has been subjected to a substantial amount of research (and much of it is encouraging) and it can be used to evaluate large numbers of students in a relatively brief period of time. The cloze procedure cannot, however, yield the rich diagnostic information that can be derived from an IRI. See Pikulski and Tobin (1982) for a fuller discussion of the cloze procedure.

Types of Informal Reading Inventories

At least four major types of IRIs can be distinguished:
1. Teacher or Reading Specialist Constructed Informal Reading Inventories, sometimes called curriculum based IRIs. This is the type of IRI that will receive the greatest attention in this publication. As the heading implies, this IRI is developed by the person who will be using it. One of its foremost characteristics is the close match between the materials used in the IRI and the materials the teacher or specialist has available for instruction. In fact, it is expected that the IRI typically will be a *sampling* from those instructional (curriculum) materials. (This accounts for the term curriculum based IRI.) The teacher who has available several levels of a basal reader might construct IRIs from each level. A teacher who is working with older, disabled readers and who has available a set

of high interest, low vocabulary materials could construct an IRI from the various levels of these materials. It is best to think of an IRI as an approach to evaluating reader performance rather than as a test or a specific piece of testing material. As such, it is an approach that can be flexibly applied to a wide variety of instructional materials. *Individual* informal reading inventory simply means that the inventory is given to only one child at a time; it is *individually* administered.

Typically, an individual IRI consists of several different activities including:

- A discussion between the examiner and child. This preliminary discussion is designed to assess the readiness of the child to read a selection in terms of the prior knowledge the child has about the topic discussed in the selection.
- The actual oral reading of those materials by the child. The examiner makes a careful record of the child's oral reading performance.
- The assessment of the child's comprehension of the orally read materials. This may be accomplished by asking the child a series of questions about the selection or by asking the child to retell all he or she remembers of what was read.
- A selection, parallel in difficulty to that read orally, is read silently by the child.
- The assessment of the child's comprehension of the silently read selection. Questioning or retelling procedures are used again.
- An evaluation of the child's ability to efficiently and rapidly locate information in the previously silently read selection. This also permits the examiner to evaluate the oral *re*reading skills of the child; that is, reading aloud material previously read silently.
- The assessment of a child's listening comprehension skills for examiners wishing to do so. When this aspect of IRIs is used, the examiner reads selections to the child and then uses questioning or retelling strategies to evaluate the child's ability to understand and interpret materials heard. Since the language processing involved in listening and reading is parallel in a number of important ways, many examiners feel comparisons of listening and reading comprehension yield useful diagnostic information.

The above steps can be repeated with selections at easier or more difficult reading levels.

Individually administered IRIs usually consist of materials at several levels of difficulty. Thus, the teacher tries to initiate the evaluation with materials the student can read easily and continues testing with materials of increasing levels of difficulty until the individual can no longer function adequately. The record of the student's performance is also evaluated for strengths and weaknesses. An individual reading inventory also may include an evaluation of the child's listening skills.

2. Basal Reader Individual Informal Reading Inventories. One manifestation of the popularity and utility of IRIs is the widespread existence of IRIs to accom-

pany basal reader series. Most of the widely used basal reader programs have available IRIs constructed from samples of their instructional materials. In this sense, they are like teacher or specialist constructed IRIs, and also curriculum based IRIs.

The form and quality of basal reader inventories vary considerably. Because of the very nature of IRIs, the user of basal reader inventories is urged to review them critically, to modify them as needed, or to discard them. Since they are informal tools, it is perfectly acceptable for a teacher to eliminate an inferior comprehension question and replace it with a better one in such an inventory. If the basal IRI seems generally sound, except for the choice of a selection at a particular level, a new selection can be chosen from the instructional materials and substituted. In many cases, a basal reader IRI serves as a good starting point for the construction of an IRI for use with that series, but modification may be necessary in order to satisfy a teacher's standards or purposes.

3. General Individual Informal Reading Inventories. Another manifestation of the popularity of IRIs is the sizeable number of inventories publishers are producing for general evaluation of reading. In their administration, and to some extent in their form, they are similar to the two types of IRIs already discussed. Their major differences are that the selections usually are not related to any particular set of instructional materials and they are not curriculum based. Authors of general inventories hope (and sometimes claim) that they can be used in conjunction with a wide variety of instructional materials. Jongsma and Jongsma (1981) briefly describe and review features of eleven of these inventories.

General IRIs are popular. First, they are convenient. They usually contain two or three supposedly parallel or alternate passages of graded materials ranging from preprimer through sixth or eighth grade level. Such passages can be used to evaluate oral reading, silent reading, and listening comprehension skills at varying levels of difficulty. All the materials needed for administering the inventory are included, often in a spiral bound booklet, with the exception of multiple copies of the forms required for recording an individual's performance. In most cases, however, these record forms are included along with the publisher's permission to duplicate them. This is a second advantage; because of the permission to duplicate record forms, these inventories become an inexpensive way to evaluate reading compared to tests requiring record forms which must be purchased for each administration. Finally, this type of IRI seems popular because some teachers and specialists seem insecure about their ability to construct their own IRIs.

The quality of these published, general IRIs varies considerably. Again, one must be critical in selecting and using them. The option exists to modify these inventories by adding or deleting questions or substituting different passages.

The use of published general inventories raises one important question: How similar are the reading skills and the level of difficulty of the published IRI to the skills and difficulty of the instruction materials intended for use based on the IRI results? On the face of it, the advantage of close correspondence, even equivalency, between the materials for testing and for teaching is lost when published general IRIs are used. There is some research evidence, however, to suggest that there is a reasonable amount of agreement in the instructional level established by a teacher constructed IRI and at least one of the general IRIs (Pikulski & Shanahan, 1982; Bristow, Pikulski, & Pelosi, 1983).

4. Teacher or Specialist Constructed Group Informal Reading Inventories. There are circumstances when evaluating children one at a time simply is not realistic. Given a large number of children who need to be placed in instruction groups, individual evaluation might take weeks. Group IRIs (described in Chapter 7) will not provide as detailed an account of each child's reading strengths and weaknesses and some aspects of reading performance (e.g., extended oral reading) will not be evaluated. However, group inventories will yield sufficient information for a teacher to make an initial instructional placement expeditiously and with reasonable accuracy. Certainly, some modification may be needed in instructional group membership based on a group IRI after the teacher has an opportunity to observe children as they respond to the challenge of their reading materials; but no reading evaluation instrument in existence is so precise that such modifications will not be needed.

Reliability and Validity of Informal Reading Inventories

The concepts of reliability and validity are almost impossible to avoid when discussing any form of evaluation. It is not the purpose of this publication to defend or critically review the reliability and validity of these instruments. Such reviews appear periodically in professional journals (McKenna, 1983; Pikulski, 1974; Pikulski & Shanahan, 1982) and should be consulted. However, it seems appropriate to point out to the user or potential user of IRIs that there are a number of unanswered questions regarding their reliability and validity, but that is also a very strong rationale for the use of this approach.

Reliability relates to consistency of results. The users of IRIs must exercise caution as there are some research reports suggesting potential problems in reliability. Allington (1978) and Page and Carlson (1975) present evidence that when different reading specialists work with the same IRI results, they make very different interpretations about where students should be placed for instruction. Their interpretations are not reliable. On the other hand, there are studies by Lamberg, Rodriguez, and Douglas (1978) and Roe and Aiken (1976) that are much more encouraging regarding the reliability of instructional decisions made from IRIs. Pikulski and Shanahan (1982) interpret the differences between the studies to reflect recency of training. If users of IRIs have worked fairly recently and have received the same form of training on the use of IRIs, it appears that reliable results can be achieved.

The strength of IRIs with respect to reliability lies in the fact that the results can and should be viewed as tentative. Results should be checked, verified, or modified based on the reading instruction that follows the use of an IRI.

Validity is the extent to which an evaluation procedure or test measures what it says it measures. Establishing the validity of reading measures is an extremely complex procedure. Critical reviews such as those cited earlier should be consulted since there are validity questions relative to the whole concept of an instructional level and the criteria for establishing reading levels that remain unsettled regarding IRIs. However, a major strength of IRIs relates to their content validity. Most other testing procedures, including standardized tests, criterion referenced tests, and even published IRIs, are composed of content from sources different from the content to which the results are to be applied. The extent to which the results derived from such measures validly apply to instructional materials is open to question. The use of an IRI, the content of which is an actual sampling of the materials from which a child might receive instruction, makes the results of an IRI a powerful and immediately useful approach to evaluation.

Conclusions

IRIs should not be thought of as tests, but as a series of strategies that can be used flexibly to help determine the level of reading material appropriately challenging for a student. They also may be used to diagnose reading strengths and weaknesses, to help a teacher more fully understand the nature of some reading problems, to allow a teacher to make informal judgments about the amount of reading progress an individual has made, and to help learners become more aware of their levels of reading ability.

Some of the characteristics of IRIs become more clearly understood when this approach to evaluation is compared and contrasted with standardized reading tests, miscue analysis, criterion referenced tests, and the cloze procedure. The utility of each of these forms of reading evaluation depends to a large degree on the purposes for which they are being used.

IRIs can take on several forms. The remainder of this publication focuses on the use of teacher or reading specialist constructed, curriculum based IRIs that are administered to one individual at a time. However, individualized inventories are also commonly prepared by publishers of basal reading programs and a substantial number of IRIs are published which are meant for use with any child, regardless of the materials being used for instruction. IRIs also can be used as group measures.

While many questions related to the reliability and validity of IRIs remain unanswered, the strength of this evaluative approach lies in the potentially close match that can exist between testing and instructional materials.

Chapter 2
Estimating Reading Levels from Informal Reading Inventories

Certainly, it is not uncommon to find children attempting to function in reading groups, unable to meet the word identification or comprehension challenges of the materials being used. Nor is it difficult to find children working "independently" on a worksheet they find bewildering in its demands. Situations such as these seem particularly distressing since Berliner (1981) reports that placing students in situations where the academic challenge was too great led to lower achievement and that such overplacement had a detrimental effect on the students' psychological makeup and attitudes as well.

It seems quite reasonable to think that at least part of the reason children are placed in reading materials that are too difficult may be the result of inappropriate evaluation techniques. The statement endorsed by the International Reading Association (cited in Chapter 1 of this publication) warns against the misuse of grade equivalent scores from standardized tests as a reference to text difficulty and, hence, as the basis for instructional placement in reading. Too often in reading instruction minimal criteria are used to judge the adequacy for a child's performance on a reading measure. Consequently, the level at which a child's performance is judged adequate for working independently, without teacher guidance, often turns out to be the level where that child encounters many problems.

In the same fashion, test results are often used to arrive at conclusions that children are ready for instruction at a particular level when, in fact, they are not. When there is too much to be accomplished through instruction and when the probability of failure is high, the child does not adequately profit from instruction and retain those things which are taught. In order to overcome these weaknesses, high standards must be used for judging a child's readiness for interacting with reading materials at various levels of difficulty. Examiners often erroneously think they are acting kindly toward children when they conclude they are capable of reading at a level higher than reading performance would warrant. While receiving a higher reading score or being placed in a higher reading group may be momentarily satisfying to a student (and the parents of that student), such a decision may set the stage for inefficient and ineffective instruction and learning and for the high probability of frustration and subsequent failure for the student.

The accurate placement of children in a sequential program of reading instruction is extremely important. While the dangers of overplacement have been stressed, it should be obvious that it would be a waste of time for both teacher and pupil, as well as limiting the potential for growth, to work at a level of material that could be easily mastered by the child independently, with no aid or guidance from a teacher.

The remainder of this chapter is devoted to discussing the definitions of and criteria for establishing an individual's independent, instructional, frustration, and listening comprehension levels. Numerical criteria are offered for estimating these levels, but it should be kept in mind that establishing a reading level is based upon qualitative interpretations with reference to these quantitative guidelines. The numerical criteria for accuracy of oral reading in context and comprehension performance should be seen only as beginning guidelines for establishing appropriate reading levels. While it will be helpful to calculate quantitative scores, the nature and severity of the errors made and the overall quality of the reading performance must be carefully reviewed by the examiner in order to draw diagnostic conclusions about the individual's reading strengths and needs and to establish reading levels. Not all professionals in reading are in agreement as to the best quantitative criteria to apply. Unfortunately, the research focused on IRIs completed to date is not conclusive; however, comprehensive reviews of that research (McKenna, 1983; Pikulski, 1974; Pikulski & Shanahan, 1982) are the bases for retaining the criteria for establishing levels that were suggested in the first (1965) edition of this publication.

In addition, the valid and reliable use of IRIs must rely upon the accurate professional judgments of the person conducting the evaluation. The accurate use of IRIs requires judgment and interpretation, not the mechanical calculation or application of scores.

Independent Reading Level

This is a level at which children can function on their own and do a virtually perfect job in responding to the printed material. The reading performance should be free from observable behaviors which are sometimes indications of difficulty—behaviors such as finger pointing, vocalization, lip movement, or other evidences of general tension in the reading situation. It should be noted that such behaviors, sometimes associated with difficulty in reading, occasionally are simply inefficient habits. They are, however, also shown by proficient readers when they encounter difficult reading materials.

At the reader's independent reading level oral reading should be done in a rhythmical fashion and in a conversational tone. At an independent level there tends to be close correspondence between what the child reads and the actual text. However, some deviations from the text are permissible and, in fact, expected. For example, even mature, skilled readers deviate from the text as they read orally. They substitute words for those printed, occasionally omit words, or sometimes add words. However, the nature of these miscues or errors is such that they do little to alter the meaning of the text. The hallmark of the miscues at the independent level is that they do not violate the syntax (grammar) of the material nor do they substantively alter the meaning of the passage.

The quantitative guideline for materials to be considered on an independent level is that they should be read with 99 percent accuracy in terms of word recognition. This does not mean merely final recognition of the words in the selection. Rather, this means that even in a situation of oral reading at sight, the child should be able to read the material accurately, making no more than one error in one hundred running words. However, if the reading is fluent, if the meaning is preserved, a few minor miscues are acceptable.

In terms of comprehension, regardless of whether the reading has been done silently or orally, the child should be able to respond accurately to questions testing for factual recall, for ability to interpret and infer, and for critical reaction to the material. In short, the child's responses should reflect the comprehension ability required for full understanding of the material. The child should be able to follow sequences of events involved in the material, discern how details relate to generalizations, note comparisons and contrasts drawn in the paragraphs, and be able to understand the organization or structure of the text being read. The quantitative guideline suggested for materials to be termed as at a child's independent level is that 90 percent of the questions should be answered accurately.

While ideally one should expect equally good performance in both oral and silent reading comprehension, some tempering of this expectation is in order. In using an IRI, the examiner asks a child questions based on one selection read orally and one read silently. Occasionally, one encounters children who become so preoccupied with their oral reading performance that their ability to understand the passage and remember what they read suffers. In such a case it might be appropriate to weigh the silent comprehension score more heavily than the oral comprehension score.

Traditionally, IRIs have used questions to evaluate comprehension; however, an acceptable alternative procedure is that of retelling. The use of retelling to evaluate comprehension involves asking children to tell all they remember about a selection just read. At an independent level, a child will be able to reflect most of the content of a selection and will reflect it in an organized fashion. Children who thoroughly understand a narrative passage generally will recount events in the order in which they occur. Retelling of expository materials at an independent level generally will reflect the text structure or organization of that material. Paragraphs which are organized with the initial presentation of a generalization followed by supporting detail usually will be retold in this manner. It is not uncommon for children to include in their retellings what are sometimes called intrusions or elaborations, information from their own backgrounds of experience which was not actually included in the selection read. Such additions are definitely to be expected if reading comprehension is viewed as an interaction between the information in the text and the information the reader brings to that text. However, these intrusions and elaborations should not be incongruous with the text information and should be somewhat limited in quantity and scope.

When applying the quantitative guidelines for determining a child's independent reading level, it is necessary that the criteria for both word identification and comprehension be met. Children who can read orally but who understand little if anything of the content of the selection are not reading at all; they are engaging in what has been called "word calling"—saying the words correctly but not understanding the meaning. This could hardly be considered reading, and therefore, achieving the desired accuracy of pronunciation does not constitute an independent level for an informal *reading* inventory. By the same token, there are some children who, in spite of serious weaknesses in word recognition skills, struggle to gain meaning from the passage and thus meet the criteria for comprehension but not word recognition. Again, it would be a mistake to term this a child's independent level. Eventually the struggle with word identification may lead the child to give up and begin to avoid reading as an independent activity.

Finally, it should be pointed out that there are factors which will dramatically influence independent level reading performance that cannot be comprehensively evaluated, even through a careful administration of an IRI. For example, while an examiner might make some inferences about the degree to which a child is self-directed in reading, self-direction cannot be adequately measured. In a sense, the ability to be self-directed with respect to reading is the sine qua non of an independent level and, unfortunately, this characteristic cannot be fully measured by an IRI or any other reading instrument. Likewise, the degree to which a child is interested in a book or its content will dramatically influence independent level reading. While the examiner might gain information about some areas of interest and lack of interest, building a comprehensive list of such areas is impossible. Here again, an IRI can provide useful, guiding information to be used by a continuously observing teacher. Neither it, nor any other reading test, can provide final answers.

Attention to the independent level can be a key factor in building progress in reading. The child, the teacher, the parents, and the librarian should be concerned with this level. All are involved in the process of selection of materials for a child's independent reading. Books bought for pleasure reading, for a personal library, should be ones that can be read with relative ease, as should reference books suggested to a child as resources for developing a project or a report. Teachers should try to make homework assignments that are at students' independent levels; otherwise, the students will be forced to rely on outside help.

Attention to the independent level is necessary if we are to provide children with opportunities to apply widely the reading skills and strategies they are being taught. All too frequently it appears that reading instruction emphasizes mastery of specific reading subskills with insufficient opportunities provided to amalgamate these skills. Children also need to be able to rapidly and accurately recognize words in order to focus their attention on the comprehension aspects of reading. Frequent, wide reading of independent level materials is the most obvious recommendation for bringing about this rapid recognition of words.

Finally, if we take seriously the admonition that as teachers we have a serious responsibility to not only teach children to read, but to create in them an appreciation of reading and a desire to read, it seems imperative that we supply them with many reading materials they can handle with facility. Frequently children are given a steady diet of difficult materials to read, and the level of difficulty prevents children from enjoying reading. It is through wide reading at the independent level that children have opportunities to apply the abilities they are developing, to learn through their own efforts, to increase the rate and flexibility of their reading—in short, to bring their reading ability to the point where it provides them with satisfaction. Only through many opportunities for independent reading will an individual become a spontaneous reader, one to whom reading is a natural part of living.

Some educators (e.g. Spache, 1976) have taken the position that the high degree of accuracy and the high standards recommended for the establishment of an independent reading level with IRIs are unnecessarily high and demanding. They argue that students will self-select highly interesting materials for independent reading and, because of this interest, will be willing and able to tolerate a relatively high level of difficulty. While there is little doubt that individuals occasionally read independently some difficult materials of high interest to them, it is unlikely they will continue to read such difficult materials over a long period of time—especially when they are being *held accountable for full understanding of the content of the materials.* In addition, the concept of an independent level described here is broader than self-selection of high interest level material. It is designed to cover assigned materials as well as self-selected. For example, can a social studies teacher assume that homework reading assignments always will be of high interest to students? It seems reasonable that a topic which is not of interest to students will have a significantly better chance of becoming an area of interest if the reader can focus attention on the content rather than struggling to meet word identification, word meaning, sentence structure, or text structure demands of the material. In this way, independent level materials appear to have the potential for extending a reader's range of interest.

Instructional Reading Level

Instructional reading level is the level at which children can be profitably instructed. They will encounter some challenge in interacting with the reading material, but these challenges should be adequately met through the help of a teacher. In order to fulfill the criteria for establishing an instructional level, children should be free from externally observable symptoms of serious difficulty. Again, as at the independent level, students should be able to orally read rhythmically and in a conversational tone. One would expect certain difficulties to arise in the course of oral reading at sight (i.e. oral reading in a situation where there was no opportunity to read the materials silently); however, when children have a chance to read the material silently first, most of these difficulties should be overcome. Consequently, oral *re*reading should be definitely improved over oral reading at sight. While the use of oral reading at sight is not advocated as an instructional procedure, it has value for diagnostic purposes. It allows for observation of the full range of difficulties children are likely to encounter, even though with extra time and effort they might be able to overcome these problems.

At an instructional level, a reader will be able to deal with most of the language-concept-comprehension demands made by the material, but there are likely to be some demands that will be beyond the child's understanding. Limitations in background of experience and vocabulary knowledge may reduce the fluency of the oral reading. As readers encounter difficulty in understanding, they lose one of the most important aids to decoding. At an independent level, readers can accomplish such understanding on their own but at an instructional level, a teacher's help and guidance are needed. A difference exists in the goals for independent and for instructional materials. Independent reading is performed to allow independent application and consolidation of previously taught skills, whereas instructional level materials are used to teach new skills or to practice (under teacher direction) newly introduced skills.

The quality of oral reading at an instructional level should be good. Deviations from the printed text will be more frequent than at an independent level and will begin to reflect limitations in decoding or word identification skills. Substitutions are likely to become more frequent and occasionally will not be semantically or even syntactically correct. However, such breakdowns in extracting meaning should be rare. At the instructional level, a characteristic which will be especially important to note is whether the reader attempts to self-correct those substitutions which alter or detract from the meaning of the passage. In one sense this is a positive sign, a clear indication that the reader is reading for meaning and actively using the context clues in the material. Nevertheless, there are some weaknesses in decoding or understanding which prevent a meaningful, acceptable initial response.

The quantitative guideline for materials to be considered on an instructional level is that they should be read with 95 percent accuracy in terms of word recognition. Again, this guideline will need to be tempered by the nature and quality of the overall oral reading performance of the reader.

Comprehension at an instructional level should be good though, again, some weaknesses may surface. If a retelling strategy is employed, a child responding to instructional level materials will reflect less content than at an independent level. The organization of the passage will be less complete and some minor misinterpretations and inaccuracies may begin to appear. If the material is to be judged instructional for the child, it is essential that the overall sense and content of the selection be retold.

Children's understanding of concepts contained in this level of materials is somewhat superficial or incomplete. Students may encounter words that are not part of their listening or speaking vocabularies. The selection may require a more nearly complete background of experience than readers possess. If faced with limitations such as those noted, children may have some minor difficulties answering questions based on material read. Because energy was expended trying to understand the materials, attention and concentration may have been strained and some facts from the story forgotten. Responses will reflect some weaknesses in manipulating or evaluating the ideas presented because the children did not fully understand the ideas. However, as indicated earlier, none of these limitations should be widespread; at an instructional level one would expect children to show a good general understanding of the material, to be able to follow the general structure of the passage, and to remember most of the content.

The quantitative guideline for performance in comprehension at an instructional level is that children should be able to answer 75 percent of the questions asked orally about silently read passages, or retell with 75 percent accuracy of understanding and interpretation.

At both independent and instructional levels, it is necessary for qualitative and quantitative guidelines to be met for both word recognition and comprehension. Serious limitations in either area will prevent the reader from mastering the reading material—the goal of good instruction. The instructional goal should be to have children capable of responding to the material independently by the time the lesson is completed. If readers begin the lesson with major limitations in either word identification or comprehension, there is little likelihood they will overcome preexisting problems.

Through direct teacher instruction at the instructional level, students will have the opportunity to build new reading and thinking abilities. Building on the foundation of previously acquired skills, children can profit from direct teaching and extend concepts, word analysis skills, and comprehension abilities. The purpose of instruction is to extend these skills through both increased range of abilities and greater depth of applicability.

Up to this point in the chapter, for sake of simplicity, we have been discussing an instructional level. In truth, with many individuals evaluated it would be a gross oversimplification to speak about an instructional level; it would be far more realistic to think in terms of an instructional range. Even in carefully structured basal reader instruction it is not uncommon to find children who have some specific instructional needs at, let us say, a third reader level. These same children have strengths which allow them to function adequately with teacher support in fourth reader level materials. The probability of even wider instructional ranges exists as one moves from one content area to another. The child who appears uninterested in natural science and who has read very little in this area may need instructional support in reading fourth reader level natural science materials, yet be capable of profiting from instruction in sixth reader level social science materials. The teacher should determine that materials within a child's instructional range can be mastered with teacher guidance and pupil interaction with the text materials. When instructional ranges have been established for a child, ongoing decisions need to be made about the level at which the teacher will work with the child. Such decisions ought to consider the skills, abilities, and psychological characteristics of the child, as well as the particular demands made by some materials. In Chapter 4 and the Appendix, illustrations show how such diagnostic information should be interpreted and translated into instructional planning.

Frustration level. The point at which the child becomes completely unable to handle reading materials is termed *frustration level.* Information as to this level will give the teacher some guidance about the kinds of material to avoid. It may also give some indication of the rate at which the child might be able to progress when taught at a proper instructional level. If a child is ready for instruction at one level and completely frustrated at the next, there are problems to be overcome at the appropriate instructional level. It is not likely this instruction will progress rapidly because of the pervasiveness of the problems. On the other hand, if there is a considerable spread between instructional and frustration levels, there is a better chance for fairly rapid progress. This spread is evidence that children can continue to use reading strategies with some effectiveness even in response to materials somewhat beyond their instructional range. This would seem to indicate the needs to be met at the instructional level, and slightly above, are not pervasive or complex. Consequently, children might be expected to work through most problems quite rapidly with the help of good instruction.

Given what has just been said, it is possible to have a gap between the instructional and frustration levels. For example, it is possible for a child to achieve an instructional level at third reader level but not to reach a frustration level until fifth. This suggests there were many skills the child was able to demonstrate when asked to read fourth reader level materials, but the distance between the demands of fourth level reading materials and the skills of the reader was too great for successful mastery of the material. As noted, the distance between the instructional and frustration levels suggests that one might expect fairly rapid progress.

When a child reaches a frustration level, behavioral indicators, frequently absent when the child was dealing with less challenging materials, begin to manifest themselves. When children have comprehension problems, discussions preceding the oral or silent reading may reveal little background for, or even some misinformation about, the topic of the selection. Predictions about the content of the selections will tend to be restricted or poorly formulated.

Oral reading at a frustration level commonly becomes arrhythmical and slow. It becomes clear that the child is reading individual words rather than thought units. Words are omitted or substitutions are made which violate the meaning or syntax of the passage, and often no attempt is made to correct the errors. At a frustration level there is a strong tendency for the reader to stop using language/context clues and to focus more attention on graphic or phonics clues to word identification.

When a retelling procedure is used, materials at a frustration level are recalled incompletely or in a rather haphazard fashion. Bits of information may be recalled, but they are not related in any logical or sequential order. Questions asked by the examiner tend to go unanswered. Finger pointing, lip movement, vocalization during silent reading, and other overt behaviors may appear. The child may look tense and distressed.

Suggested numerical criteria for the frustration level include comprehension of 50 percent or less *or* word recognition of 90 percent or less. A frustration level is established if the child's performance falls below either of these numerical criteria. Serious limitations in either word identification or comprehension will constitute a frustration level.

Listening comprehension level. This is the highest level at which children can satisfactorily understand materials read to them. The listening comprehension level can serve as a reflection of the vocabulary, other language skills, concepts, and background of experience the reader possesses. While there are some differences, to a very great extent the language/thinking skills required for listening comprehension are virtually the same as those required for reading comprehension (Sticht & James, 1984). In reading, however, there is a need for visual word identification (decoding). The listening comprehension level can be thought of as the level at which the reader would be able to perform reading comprehension activities if word recognition skills were adequately developed. Criteria for judgment of adequacy of listening comprehension are similar to comprehension in establishing the reading instructional level. If retelling is used it should possess the qualities indicative of comprehension at an instructional level and students should be able to answer at least 75 percent of the questions asked about materials read to them. The necessity for the examiner to rephrase and simplify the language level or for the children to answer in a lower level of language would indicate a lack of full comprehension.

In some respects the listening comprehension level suggests the level at which children should be reading based on their language development, thinking skills, and backgrounds of experience. Some writers speak of this as capacity level—the highest level children could be expected to attain if decoding skills were developed. The term *capacity* carries unfortunate connotations of setting limits for children and thus is not used in this volume. Our position as authors is that teachers of reading have the responsibility of determining on what level children are functioning and moving them forward rather than trying to determine whether they have reached their capacity.

Knowing children's listening comprehension levels in relationship to their instructional levels can be informative diagnostically. There is a substantial difference between the child who has both an instructional and listening comprehension level at second reader and the one who achieves a reading instructional level at second reader but a listening comprehension level at fourth. In the case of the youngster whose instructional and listening levels were established at second reader level, it would appear that, before additional reading progress can be made, general language skills and concept attainment will need to be improved. Perhaps vocabulary or background of experience needs to be expanded, or the child needs instruction in dealing with more complex syntactic forms, or specific instruction needs to be offered as to how to make inferences or draw conclusions. On the other hand, the child whose instructional level is at second but whose listening comprehension is at fourth already possesses substantial language and thinking skills that can be applied to reading. In this latter case, it is quite possible limitations or inefficiencies in word recognition skills interfere with the extent to which these language skills can be applied to reading materials. It is also possible the child needs instruction in features specific to written language, such as correctly interpreting or meaningfully grouping words into phrases (Horowitz & Samuels, 1985). It is even possible the child has developed a concept of reading where he or she does not realize reading requires the use of the same language and thinking abilities used in other language/thinking situations.

Summary of Criteria for Reading Levels

The following chart summarizes the primary qualitative and numerical criteria for estimating independent, instructional, and frustration reading levels.

Independent

The level at which readers can function on their own and do a virtually perfect job responding to printed material.

Qualitative Indicators	*Quantitative Criteria*
Oral Reading	
fluent, rhythmical	99% accuracy*
absence of behaviors associated with reading difficult material	
few deviations from print; deviations do not affect meaning	
Comprehension (Oral and Silent)	
answers to questions or retellings reflect full understanding of material	90% accuracy*
balanced merger of prior knowledge and text information	
retellings well organized; reflect organization of text	

*Both oral reading and comprehension criteria must be met.

Instructional

The level at which readers will profit maximally from teacher directed instruction in reading.

Qualitative Indicators	Quantitative Criteria
Oral Reading	
fluent, rhythmical; few indicators of difficulty	95-98% accuracy*
few deviations from print that affect meaning; deviations from meaning are self-corrected	
near absence of behaviors associated with reading difficult material	
oral rereading improved over oral reading at sight	
Comprehension (Oral and Silent)	
meets most language and background of experience challenges of the material and integrates prior knowledge with text information	75-89%*
answers to questions and retellings reflect good understanding for and memory of the material	
retellings basically reflect organization of text; no serious intrusions or distortions	
shows the ability to manipulate and critically respond to ideas in the text, though minor misinterpretations may occur	

*Both oral reading and comprehension criteria must be met.

Frustration

The level at which reading materials become so difficult that children cannot successfully respond to them, even with teacher direction/guidance.

Qualitative Indicators	Quantitative Criteria
Oral Reading	
slow, labored, nonfluent	90% or less
deviations from text affect meaning	
appearance of behaviors (e.g. finger pointing, head movement) associated with reading very difficult material	
oral rereading is not improved over oral reading at sight	
Comprehension (Oral and Silent)	
prereading discussions suggest weak language skills and background knowledge for understanding content of selections	50% or less
answers to questions or retellings reveal lack of sensitivity to organization of materials, poor memory for content, and misinterpretations of content selection	

Conclusions

Students of IRIs sometimes overemphasize the precision of the quantitative criteria cited for establishing levels from an inventory. As indicated earlier, quantitative criteria serve as reasonable starting points for establishing levels, but they must not be slavishly applied. The behavioral criteria listed in the discussion of each level also must be taken into consideration. It will become apparent in Chapter 4 and the Appendix that, while all oral reading errors are weighed equally in calculating the word recognition score, not all detract equally from the reading performance. The skills and experience of the examiner must be brought into play in interpreting the scores in light of the child's total performance on an IRI.

As a check, it is recommended that after making an attempt to establish the reading levels on an IRI, the examiner should look at the child's performance on the inventory and ask the following questions.

1. Of the level set for an *Independent Level:* Would I feel comfortable in recommending books at this level of difficulty to this child for pleasure or independent study reading? Is it likely the child will master the content of the reading material without assistance?

2. Of the *Instructional Level:* Would I as a teacher be comfortable working with this child as he or she reads materials at this level of challenge? Is the level of material challenging enough to encourage growth in reading skills, yet not so difficult that it will be virtually impossible for the child to master the material, even with teacher help?

3. Of the *Frustration Level:* Does this level of material present so much difficulty that the gap is so wide between what the child can do and what needs to be done in order to master the material that even with teacher help mastery will not occur?

Anyone using informal reading inventories should keep in mind that establishing levels from these instruments should serve as the basis for good instructional planning; establishing levels is not an academic exercise of applying numerical criteria. Unless the levels established for an IRI provide practical guidance for classroom or clinical instruction, there is no justification for their use.

Chapter 3

Administering, Recording, and Scoring Individual Informal Reading Inventories

Overview

An individual informal reading inventory is best thought of as a systematic sampling of reading behavior under structured conditions with an emphasis placed on evaluating and better understanding the overall, integrated reading performance of the person to whom the inventory is administered. However, in order to better understand the administration of the IRI it is helpful to think of sections, parts, or phases of the inventory.

As suggested in earlier chapters, IRIs offer opportunities to evaluate 1) pupil readiness for reading certain selections, 2) oral reading skills, 3) comprehension of orally read materials, 4) comprehension of silently read materials, 5) efficiency in locating specific information in a text and orally rereading a portion which previously had been read silently, and 6) ability to comprehend connected text materials heard rather than read. Used flexibly, IRIs can appraise a child's ability to use the table of contents, glossary, subject index, footnotes, source and recency of material, and to interpret all of the pictorial and graphic aids normally included as part of a text. Because the establishment of reading levels is usually one of the expected and most frequently sought outcomes of the administration, the inventory consists of at least two passages—one to be read orally and one silently—and a list of comprehension questions for each. Several sets of such materials representing various levels of difficulty are included. The normal steps followed in administering an IRI are:

1. The examiner explores the child's readiness for reading a selection of text and guides the establishment of a purpose for oral reading.
2. The child reads one selection (at a specified level of difficulty) orally, and the examiner records the performance.
3. The examiner evaluates comprehension of the materials read orally by asking questions and/or using a retelling strategy or some other technique.
4. The child develops readiness and motivation for reading a selection silently (at the same level of difficulty).
5. The child then reads a selection silently and the examiner observes the child's behavior during this reading. This selection is at the same level of difficulty as the one read orally, as indicated in step 2.

6. The examiner evaluates comprehension through asking the child to retell what he or she read, by asking the child questions based on the material read silently, or by using other techniques designed to assess comprehension of what was read.
7. The examiner asks the child, for a newly established purpose, to locate and orally reread a portion of the selection recently read silently.

The same set of steps is then usually repeated with selections at a different level of difficulty. If the child did well with the first selections read, materials at a more difficult level are presented; if the child did poorly on the first selections read, easier level materials may be used. The examiner continues testing until sufficient data are gathered to establish independent, instruction, and frustration reading levels. Then a final step in an IRI can take place.

8. The examiner reads a selection to the child and asks questions based on the content of the selection in order to determine the child's ability to understand the material read. It is usually necessary to evaluate listening comprehension skills at more than one level of difficulty in order to establish a listening comprehension level.

The remainder of this chapter is devoted to an in-depth look at each of the listed steps in the administration of individual informal reading inventories.

Preparing for Testing

The examiner who lacks extensive experience in using IRIs will need to do a great deal of preparation before meeting with the individual to be tested. The "shorthand" system needed to record all significant elements of observed behavior during the testing must be mastered to the point where it can be employed quickly and accurately. Materials for the child to read and materials on which the examiner records observations of behavior must be assembled and in order. A place should be arranged to test the child in an atmosphere relatively quiet and free from distraction. Without thorough preparation before testing begins, testing time will be unnecessarily lengthened, perhaps to the point of raising questions about the reliability (and consequently the validity) of the results due to the child becoming bored or tired.

Establishing Rapport

The cooperation of the person being examined is necessary if the IRI is to give valid and reliable results. Consequently, rapport must be established between pupils and examiner. The examiner should briefly explain the testing procedures to be used. It is important for pupils to have some understanding of the method to be used to evaluate their accomplishments and needs in the reading area. It is best to keep the explanations general and simple, avoiding technical terms. It is also wise to explain that testing is done to get information about children's reading so you will be able to help students develop better reading skills. Finally, pupils should be told to expect to face tasks of increasing difficulty. They should know that an effort will be made to begin with materials which may not seem challenging to enable readers to demonstrate their skills and understanding in the area of reading, but that materials will become more difficult so they can go as far as their abilities will allow.

It is important throughout the administration of the IRI for the examiner to try to set a tone which has a balance of friendliness, support, structure, and control. Children should realize they are expected to put forth their best efforts, yet should feel comfortable and relaxed. At the same time, in order to accomplish the testing within a reasonable period of time, it is necessary for the examiner to be in control of the situation and maintain a reasonable amount of structure. Keep in mind that the basic purpose of administering the IRI is to collect as much information as possible about the reading strategies and behaviors of the children being tested and not to directly help individuals learn new information or master new material. Examiners who spend most of their time as teachers sometimes have difficulty in this regard, wanting to correct errors and to guide children toward a correct response. Time spent efficiently focused on acquiring diagnostic information will have long range benefits for teaching and learning.

While rapport is being established, there are many different ways the examiner can informally appraise the child's oral language facility and general background knowledge. As they engage in informal conversation, the examiner can detect any actual defects in speech; appraise the degree of spontaneity in informal situations; determine the child's ability to respond to specific questions; draw some conclusions about the range of general prior knowledge the child possesses; and get some rough measure of the maturity level of the child's vocabulary, sentence structure, and pronunciation. While all of this is going on, much can be learned about the child's attitudes and interests in reading. All of these conclusions must be tentatively drawn, although eventually they will be significant in the total evaluation of strengths and weaknesses observed during the reading performance.

Determining the Level at Which to Begin

Determining the level at which to begin the administration of an IRI is often an area of great concern to those new to this technique. They often seem to want hard and fast rules; instead, there are flexible guidelines.

Obviously, the more the examiner knows about the child, the more accurate he or she can be in estimating a reasonable starting level. Cumulative record information, previous test data, the level at which the child is presently being instructed, and even the child's own evaluation of his or her reading abilities often will give valuable clues as to where to begin. As a rule of thumb, it is wise to begin testing at least one level below the child's estimated instructional reading level. If it is impossible to estimate such a level, common sense must prevail. If the testing is being done because the teacher is not quite sure the child fits into the presently assigned reading group, beginning one level lower than present placement makes sense. If a third grade child is being tested because it appears that he or she has a serious reading problem, it would be reasonable to begin the IRI at the easiest level available.

Another reasonable way to estimate where to begin administering an IRI is to make the decision based on the results of an individual word recognition test. (The nature and use of individual word recognition tests are discussed in Chapter 5.) Such tests can be quickly administered. They are frequently given at the same time as an IRI because they can add information for diagnosing the nature of a child's reading problem. If such a test is used, it is recommended it be administered before the IRI. A reasonable procedure for determining where to begin administering the reading inventory is at least one level lower than that at which the child first encountered difficulty on the word recognition test. The one situation where this might not be suitable would be when there is reason to believe the child has considerable difficulties with comprehension. In this case, begin at a lower level so as to present more reasonable comprehension demands on the initially administered selection.

Exploring Readiness for Reading and Establishing a Purpose for Reading

Once the starting level has been determined, the procedures at each level are the same. Before any reading is done, readiness for the particular selection should be explored and developed. When illustrations are part of the informal inventory, they may be sufficient stimulus for initiating discussion. This prereading discussion will yield valuable information about the vocabulary and background of experience the individual brings to the selection. Since comprehension is the result of an interaction between what the reader already knows and what is presented in the reading materials, it is important to know what the reader brings to the topic. In the course of this readiness, a purpose for reading should be established. In some cases, the purposes can be quite general, such as, "Read to find out if the selection agrees with what you know about this topic." In other cases, the examiner may wish to establish a more specific purpose. The examiner must be careful not to inadvertently use any of the key vocabulary used in the selection or explain ideas contained therein, since this would inhibit the opportunity to measure accurately the extent to which the child gained an understanding of the selection through reading. Instead, some orientation should be given which will give the child a reason for reading. The examiner must keep in mind that the purpose at this point is to *test,* not to teach.

Oral Reading

After exploring readiness and establishing a purpose for reading, the selection designed for oral reading at sight is read aloud by the child in order to accom-

158048

plish the established purpose. The examiner is encouraged to time the reading, using a stopwatch. Care should be taken to use the stopwatch in an inconspicuous way since some children are upset when being timed.

As the child reads orally, the examiner must make an accurate record of the exact way in which the selection was read. Each hesitation, repetition, or error should be recorded and any significant overt behavior noted. For example, if there is need for examiner help with pronunciation of words, this is given with the exact nature of such help recorded. If the reader does not actually ask for help, it is probably best to wait at least five seconds before helping with the pronunciation of a word because of the need to evaluate as fully as possible the strategies a child will use in trying to deal with the reading material. Waiting a long time can become unnecessarily disruptive unless it is apparent the reader is still actively working out the pronunciation. Before administering an IRI for diagnostic purposes, the examiner should have considerable practice supervised by an experienced examiner or instructor. Recording oral reading performances with a tape recorder, as well as in the written form, is a valuable self-training procedure. It is sobering to learn how easy it is to fail to record some part of the oral reading performance. At the same time permission is secured for doing the testing, permission for the taping should be obtained from the child and the child's parent or guardian.

Teachers using IRIs find it helpful to develop a shorthand for use in recording all significant elements of the behavior noted during the administration. Rapid, accurate recording is necessary since in the inventory the child's oral reading of a selection is never interrupted for recording purposes. The examiner experiences few problems in recording responses at the independent and instructional levels, where symptoms of difficulty are at a minimum. However, as the selections become more difficult for the examinee, these symptoms multiply and it becomes increasingly complex for the examiner to keep pace with the reader and still note all of the errors and comments made as well as the behavior manifested. It is often diagnostically helpful to record the amount of time it took the child to complete the reading.

The following suggested recording style, once mastered, will speed up this process and make possible a consistently accurate re-creation of the test responses at a later date. However, personal comfort with the shorthand system used is more important than is uniformity from examiner to examiner. Those who are just beginning to use IRIs, but who already have mastered a shorthand system for recording oral reading, can use that system or modify it.

System for Recording Oral Reading at Sight: Reading Inventories

Recording Symbol		Behavior Noted
HM	-	head movement
FP	-	finger pointing
PC	-	use of picture clues
↑↓	-	rising or falling inflection
<u>was</u>	-	repetition
was / ~~saw~~	-	substitution
was ✓ / ~~saw~~	-	self-correction
~~was~~	-	omission
the/man	-	pause (one per second)
WXW	-	word by word
same / the ∧ big man	-	insertion
(was)	-	examiner help given
✗	-	punctuation ignored

In addition, all other pertinent behavioral symptoms and comments should be noted. The following illustrates the system for recording the oral reading.

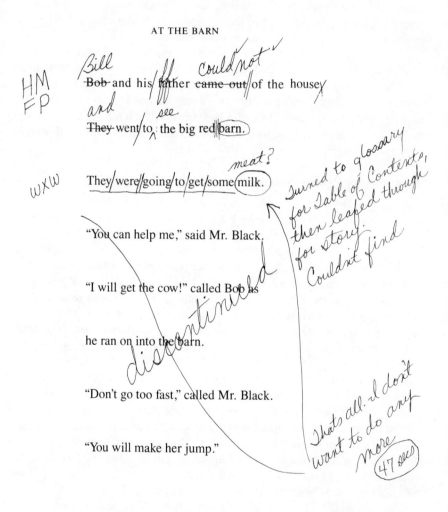

AT THE BARN

In this case, after establishing a purpose for reading, the examiner asked the child to locate in the book the story "about a farm"; the resultant method employed (that of beginning with the glossary) was noted as were the subsequent behaviors and the result. The discussion which followed suggested the child brought to the reading a considerable background of experience and vocabulary related to farms.

The actual reading began with a substitution of *Bill* for *Bob,* a slight pause and then an initial consonant attack on *father,* followed by a correct pronunciation of the word. Next came two substitutions (*could not* for *came out*) which were corrected by repetition after a two second pause. No pause occurred at the period at the end of the first sentence. In the second sentence, in addition to inappropriate pauses and a substitution of *and* for *they, see* was inserted and, after an extended pause, the word *barn* was given by the examiner. By the third line the child's oral reading had deteriorated to a word by word performance. The child further substituted *meat* for *milk,* but in a questioning tone, and the examiner said the word. The entire line was then repeated with the final word correctly recognized in this reading. This was followed by the reader's refusal to continue, as indicated in the margin of the illustration. Both finger pointing and head movement were evidenced during the reading. The entire performance, from the initial substitution to the final repetition, took forty-seven seconds, a reading rate of thirty-one words per minute.

Assessing Comprehension of Orally Read Materials

As soon as the oral reading is completed, the examiner attempts to assess the degree to which the content of the selection was understood and remembered. The child does not have access to the reading materials during this time. It is usually best if the examiner casually removes the material from the child and turns it upside down on the testing table after the reading has been completed.

There are several ways in which the understanding and retention of content can be evaluated. The more traditional method used in IRIs is to ask a series of questions prepared prior to the time of examination. The examiner asks these questions orally and the child responds orally. When questions are used, they should not be substantially rephrased during the evaluation; such rephrasing often has the effect of prompting or leading the child. It is important for the examiner to keep in mind that, at this time, the purpose is to evaluate the child's comprehension and not to teach. If a question is answered incorrectly, this does not mean the examiner should help the child arrive at the right answer. Instead, the examiner should go on to the next question. If after careful consideration the examiner decides a question was unfair, poorly worded, or misunderstood, this should be taken into consideration when reading levels are established. The examiner should also take whatever steps are necessary to revise, replace, or simply eliminate poor questions before the inventory is readministered.

Responses to the comprehension questions should be recorded verbatim wherever possible. If such recording is not done, the immediate reaction to the adequacy of the response is often in question; use of a tape recorder eliminates such concerns. In addition, the following abbreviations are used in recording comprehension performance:

Q—The examiner judges the child's answer to be incomplete or ambiguous, and probes or questions further: "Tell me more." "Can you tell me more?" "Tell me what you mean by...."

DK—Don't know. The child indicated not knowing the answer to a question.

A second major strategy for evaluating comprehension is the use of a retelling strategy. After the completion of the reading, the examiner simply says to the child, "Tell me all you can remember from what you just read." To achieve reliability in the use of this procedure, especially with children beyond the primary levels, the tape recording of responses is necessary since some children will quickly give much verbal information. In the use of retelling strategy, some children will stop responding before they have related all they remember. Therefore, unless the retelling has been judged to be complete, the examiner should encourage the child to tell anything else remembered about the selection just read.

A combination of the use of questioning and retelling strategies is possible. For example, some examiners prefer to prepare a list of questions, but to begin by asking the child to recount all that is remembered. The examiner then asks only those questions with answers not reflected in the retelling. Thus, there is great flexibility possible in evaluating a child's comprehension in an IRI. The examiner will need to take into consideration that different procedures evaluate different aspects of comprehension. For example, questions prompt or aid comprehension, whereas retellings call for unaided recall of the information.

Some beginning users of IRIs are distressed at the lack of definity in the guidelines offered here for the evaluation of comprehension. "Which is the best way to evaluate it?" they ask. It would be misleading to pretend there is a best way. There is much to be said in favor of the use of a retelling strategy. There is growing evidence (Marshall & Glock, 1978-1979; Meyer & Rice, 1984) to suggest that an important aspect of reading comprehension is the reader's ability to discern the relationship among the statements within a paragraph. For example, some paragraphs are organized so ideas are compared and contrasted; others depend on the sequential presentation of information. While it seems possible for a reader to discern such organization and not be able to verbalize it, there is no question but what the reader whose retelling reflects the organization inherent in a paragraph did discern it. Illustrations of how the structure of text can be reflected in a child's retelling are offered in Chapter 4 and the Appendix.

The disadvantage of a retelling strategy is that more examiner judgment is required to evaluate student responses than is required in the use of a questioning strategy. While the use of questions does not free an examiner from diagnostic interpretations, most feel it is easier to judge the correctness of the responses to the questions and then to calculate the percentage of correct responses for each passage. Some examiners feel they achieve the advantage of both techniques by first employing a retelling strategy and then asking the child questions which depend on information not reflected in the child's original retelling. In some cases, children's retelling records will reflect that they have integrated information from the selection, have combined text information with background of experience, and have inferred relationships among facts in the selection. On the other hand, some children tend to stick to the facts presented and do little elaboration. For the latter type of youngster, it would be wise to ask those questions requiring elaboration, integration, and inferencing in order to determine whether the child can engage in these important aspects of the reading process.

Illustrations of the use of retelling and questioning strategies, as well as a combination of questioning and retelling, are included in Chapter 4 and the Appendix.

Preparation for Silent Reading

When the comprehension check on the reading of the first selection (the one read orally) is completed, readiness should be established for reading the second selection. Again, a purpose must be set for the reading. This time the child is being prepared to read silently a second selection approximately at the same level of difficulty as the one just read orally.

Observing the Silent Reading

The examiner should observe carefully during the silent reading, keeping a record of the time required for the reading as well as noting any signs of difficulty or specific reactions to the material. The demands made on the examiner during this phase of the inventory are not as taxing as during the oral reading performance; nonetheless, careful observation is essential if the child's reading performance is to be fully interpreted.

In order to facilitate the recording of observations made during silent reading, the following "shorthand" system is suggested.

Silent Reading

Recording Symbol		Behavior Noted
PC	-	use of picture clues
LM	-	lip movement
HM	-	head movement
FP	-	finger pointing
V	-	vocalization
(was)	-	examiner help given

Assessing Comprehension of Silently Read Materials

Evaluation of comprehension on silently read selections can be administered in the same fashion used for the oral reading at sight. The same options and procedures exist for evaluating comprehension.

Oral Rereading

After completion of the comprehension check of the silently read material, a new purpose should be established for orally rereading a portion of the selection previously read silently. This rereading serves at least three specific purposes. It provides: 1) a gauge of the child's ability to skim for the relocation of specific information; 2) a measure of ability to read for a specific purpose and to stop when that purpose has been satisfied; and 3) an index of the ability to profit from previous silent reading of the material, and thus improve the fluency of oral rereading performance over oral reading at sight at the same level of difficulty. Improvement in fluency is to be expected in all selections ranging from just above the child's independent level through the level preceding the frustration level.

The oral rereading performance should be recorded in the same manner as the oral reading at sight, using the same recording symbols. The abbreviation ORR is often used in the margin of the recording form to designate that part of the selection actually read by the child. In addition, it is important to record some comments about the relative ease or difficulty the readers experienced in locating the part of the selection needed to satisfy the purpose established for rereading. The strategy used to locate the information also should be noted. For example, did readers remember and, therefore, rapidly locate the information? Did they skim the material to locate the information? Did they start at the beginning of the selection and read word by word until the information was located?

Discontinuing Testing of Reading

The procedures described are followed with sets of materials of varying levels of difficulty. In some cases, if testing is initiated at too challenging a level, it is recommended the examiner immediately drop to a level where a relatively perfect performance is anticipated in order to establish an independent level. Then testing can be continued through levels of increasing difficulty, following the same procedures previously described, until a frustration level has been reached. When this occurs, the reading inventory has been completed.

Evaluating Listening Comprehension

The process of determining the highest level at which children can understand materials read to them is usually begun at the level following the one at which frustration in reading was reached. In this process, the examiner again develops a readiness for the reading of the selection and sees that a purpose is established, just as was done when the children actually read the materials. In this case, however, after a purpose is established, the reading is done by the examiner. When the examiner finishes reading a selection, listening comprehension is evaluated in a manner similar to that used for measuring the children's reading comprehension — through use of retelling or questioning strategies or a combination of the two. This process is continued at successively higher levels until students fail to maintain a level of 75 percent accuracy in comprehension as assessed by a questioning strategy or until the examiner judges that an incomplete understanding or a serious misinterpretation of the selection is reflected in retelling. When difficulties with concept development, limited prior knowledge, or language comprehension in general are at the root of the reading problem, children may be able to do no better in the listening comprehension test than when they were doing the reading. In such cases, it may be necessary to use alternate selections at lower levels to establish a listening comprehension level. Alternate passages are needed to evaluate listening comprehension in the commonly encountered situation where both regular paragraphs above an instructional level were used in establishing a student's frustration level.

Calculating Scores for Oral Reading and Comprehension Performances

Although nearly all the behavioral symptoms suggested as indications of difficulty with a selection are positively related to word perception skills, only four of these are usually counted in computing the word recognition score: substitutions, insertions, omissions, and requests for examiner aid. Even if the child returns and corrects a substitution, insertion, or omission by rereading the text, it remains a scoreable error. The clinician should count the number of such errors and compute a percent score by dividing this number by the total number of words in the selection as shown in the sample which follows. When the resultant quotient is subtracted from 100, an oral reading accuracy percent score is obtained for the selection. This score should be clearly recorded on the page for each oral reading selection employed in the administration of the inventory.

Similarly, when questions are used to evaluate comprehension, the comprehension score for *each* selection at every level of materials used is computed by dividing the number of questions answered correctly by the total number of questions asked. This assumes that each question carries the same numerical weight in the inventory. When questions are included which require multiple responses, partial credit is usually given and included on a fractional basis in this total. These scores should be recorded on a summary sheet for comprehension of both orally and silently read passages and averaged for a total comprehension score at each level of material.

When only a retelling strategy is used, the examiner must use considerable judgment in determining whether the child's responses suggested whether the passage was at an independent, instructional, or frustration level. No one to date has suggested widely adopted or well supported numerical criteria for judging the adequacy of student retelling of selections. Procedures are currently being used experimentally to calculate the amount of information contained in text materials, for determining whether such information is more central and more peripheral in nature, and to determine how various portions of text are interrelated. It seems somewhat premature, however, to recommend these for widespread practical use. One fear is that the relative complexity of such procedures would discourage the use of IRIs. Therefore, when a retelling strategy is used, the examiner must compare the content of the pupil's responses with the content of the text and ask: Is the level of challenge of this material such that it would be best for the student to deal with it independently? Would it be best used under teacher direction or does it appear to be too challenging for this student?

Scoring comprehension questions used to evaluate listening skills follows the same procedures as those used to evaluate reading comprehension, though there is usually only one selection per level administered; therefore, scores are obviously not averaged.

Illustration for Scoring Oral Reading Performance

Primer Level: Oral at Sight   64 words

AT THE BARN

94%

Bob and his father came out of the house.

They went to see the big red barn.

They were going to get some milk.

"You can help me," said Mr. Black.

cows

"I will get the cow," called Bob as

he ran on into the barn.

so

"Don't go too fast," called Mr. Black.

"You will make her jump."

"I will not go too fast," said Bob.

$$64 \overline{)4.000} \quad .062 \text{ error rate}$$
$$384$$
$$160$$
$$128$$
$$32$$

$$\begin{array}{r} 100\% \\ -6 \\ \hline 94\% \end{array}$$

good rhythm, expression

38"

The illustration shown provides an opportunity to review the symbols used to record oral reading performance and to work through the calculation of word recognition in context score.

In the first line the child hesitated for so long before the word *house* that it was necessary for the examiner to supply the word. The child paused for about two seconds before the word *barn* in line two. In line three, the child paused before the word *milk* and then repeated the entire phrase *they were going to get some*. The word *milk* was then identified correctly. The fourth line was read with no difficulty or altering of the text. In the fifth line of text, the child read *cows* for *cow*, but the check above the word indicates that the child spontaneously corrected (without examiner help) the word *cow*. On the next line, the child also omitted the word *on*. In the seventh line the word *so* was substituted for the word *too*. No errors or alterations in text occurred in the rest of the selection.

As indicated earlier, only four alterations of text are counted as errors when calculating the word recognition in context score: substitutions, insertions, omissions, and requests for examiner aid. Even if the child spontaneously corrects an error, it is still counted when calculating the score. In this text there is one examiner prompt, one substitution that is spontaneously corrected, one omission, and one substitution. The total number of scored errors, 4, is then divided by the total number of words, 64, to calculate the percentage of error, .062; this subtracted from 100, gives the word recognition accuracy score, 94 percent.

While the purpose of this chapter is not to discuss interpretation, the recording of this reading (used to illustrate scoring procedures) is a good illustration of how important it is to look at the total oral reading performance and not just the quantitative score. While the score of 94 percent falls just short of the criterion for instruction, the nature of the reading strongly suggests the possibility that the child might profit from instruction at this level *if comprehension is acceptable*. Further, with the exception of one examiner prompt, all other scoreable errors were relatively minor, sparked the need for self-correction, or did little to detract from the meaning of the passage. While an examiner would need to look carefully at this child's performance at preprimer and first reader levels, based on just this level, the oral reading performance seems satisfactory for instructional purposes. It is important to note that the oral reading, obviously excepting the pauses to figure out *barn* and *milk,* was noted by the examiner to be expressive and to have "good rhythm."

It is recommended that decimal points not be used when reporting scores from IRIs. Inexperienced examiners sometimes indicate that the word recognition score for the second reader level of an IRI is, for example, 95.3 percent. Decimal points imply highly calibrated, finely tuned measuring instruments. When working with results from IRIs (and virtually all educational tests), it is more realistic to avoid the use of decimal points.

Illustration for Scoring Comprehension Performance

✓How do you know Bob and his father had not been outside? *They came out of the house*

✓Where had Bob and his father been? ✓
In their house

✓Where were they going? ✓
To the barn

Comp 80%

✓What did they want to get? ✓
Some milk from the cow

✓In what were they going to put the milk? (picture clue) *a pail*

✗ What was Bob's last name? *I forget... It told his father's name, but I forget*

✗ Did Bob expect to milk the cow? How do you know? *yes He went right to the barn Q to milk the cow*

✓How did Bob feel about being allowed to help? How do you know? *liked it Q most boys would Q He came right away when his father told him he could help*

✓What warning did Mr. Black give Bob?
not to go real fast

✓How do you know Mr. Black was afraid Bob might scare the cow?
He yelled at him to slow up or she'd jump

On the comprehension check, the child responded freely and showed ability to handle various types of questions. One bit of necessary information was forgotten for the inference about the boy's name — the father's name. However, the child made it clear that if the information had been remembered, the inference could have been made. The other error seemed to be one of failing to realize that the boy showed no signs of expecting to help until he was told he could, and then he went to bring the cow to his father rather than to milk her himself.

Conclusions

While informal reading inventories should be used flexibly and their administration varied to satisfy the purposes for which they are being used, certain procedures and sequences typically are employed. Usually, two parallel passages are used at each level of difficulty; one to evaluate oral reading and the other to evaluate silent reading. In some cases, a third selection at that same level of difficulty is used to evaluate listening comprehension skills.

When an IRI is used to comprehensively evaluate reading skills, readiness for reading a selection, oral reading performance, comprehension of orally read material, silent reading performance, comprehension of silently read material, and oral rereading performance are evaluated. If the examiner wishes to establish independent, instructional, and frustration reading levels, a series of passages that vary in difficulty should be used.

It is essential for a user of an IRI to be able to note relevant behavior during the administration of the inventory and to accurately record such behaviors; otherwise, reliable and valid interpretations of an individual's reading performance are impossible.

Chapter 4
Diagnostically Interpreting the Results of Informal Reading Inventories

A major strength of informal reading inventories is that they sample a wide variety of reading skills in a realistic, natural way. The administration of an IRI allows the examiner to observe children reading in a form similar to that used in school. Because of the wide varieties of reading tasks sampled, IRIs are rich in diagnostic information.

The second chapter of this book focused on the nature of reading levels and showed some of the practical, global information to be derived from an IRI. However, while knowledge of reading levels is extremely useful, it does not give a teacher or reading specialist information about a student's specific reading skill strengths and weaknesses. The third chapter described in greater detail the nature and structure of IRIs and explained how they are administered and scored. Those descriptions and explanations provide a framework for a more detailed look at the results of an IRI in order to determine the strong and weak aspects of student approaches to the various aspects of reading. The possible areas of interpretation seem almost limitless; therefore, this chapter is not comprehensive. Instead, it should provide an introduction to the rich and useful diagnostic information to be derived from an IRI. The Appendix provides three case illustrations of diagnostic interpretation, with respect to setting levels and, more specifically, reading strengths and weaknesses. It is recommended that it be read immediately after the reading of this chapter since it will afford an opportunity to check your understanding of how qualitative and diagnostic information from an IRI is used.

The remainder of the chapter is devoted to a discussion of the major sections of an IRI and the types of information to be derived from each section. The headings used here are the same as those used in the previous chapter which described the administration of IRIs.

Exploring Readiness for Reading and Establishing a Purpose for Reading

Any evaluation of an individual's reading performance will be incomplete unless the examiner evaluates the performance in light of what the reader brought to the text to be read. Unfortunately, many examiners use the readiness/purpose setting phase of an IRI either superficially or not at all. One possible reason for underuse of this phase of an IRI is that it requires considerable flexibility and inventiveness on the part of the examiner. While the examiner might begin by showing the child an illustration that accompanies a selection or indicate to the child the topic of that selection, few guidelines are provided regarding follow up questions, if such are needed. This chapter and the illustrations in the Appendix should provide some additional guidance for this aspect of using an IRI.

A crucial aspect of evaluating a child's reading performance does involve evaluating the concepts, background of experience, and language skills brought to the selection to be read. While the readiness purpose setting phase of an IRI yields a wide variety of information, probably its most valuable aspect is its ability to reflect a sampling of the language and concept development of the child relative to the topics of the selections to be read. Both decoding and comprehension performance will be affected by the relevant language skills and concepts a reader possesses.

Effect on decoding. The benefits of rich language skills and background of experience are likely to have their greatest effect on decoding performance beyond approximately third reader level. Many reading materials at beginning levels (traditionally through approximately third reader level) are carefully designed to use words from the listening/speaking vocabulary of most children. Reading materials beyond these levels frequently include less commonly used words which may not be in the listening/speaking vocabulary of some children. Unfortunately, aspects of decoding such as "rules" for dividing more challenging words into syllables, correctly representing vowel sounds, and placing syllabic stress appropriately are far from perfect. Knowledge regarding some of these facets of decoding is usually useful in helping the reader to approximate the pronunciation of a printed word unfamiliar to that reader. This is usually sufficient for getting readers close enough to recognize the word *if it is one they have heard before.* For example, a child who apparently was not familiar with the printed form of the word *angry* used letter-sound associations and some knowledge of syllabication to say the following as she tried to pronounce the word. She said, "an/gri – an-gri – oh, angry!" Her first attempt broke the word into syllables and applied reasonable letter-sound associations to the letters representing each of the syllables. Next, the child blended the separate syllables into a word that was nonsense because of a failure to treat *ng* as a digraph and because of shifting but still misrepresenting the association for *y* in this word. However, her third response of "Oh, *angry!*" made it clear that the sounds and syllabication attempts she had made had taken her close enough to a word she had heard before to allow her to decode it successfully. It is not likely that the decoding would have been successful if *angry* had not been a word she had heard and spoken before.

Compare the performance just described with the situation of a child who knows little about camels and who comes across the following sentence: "Bactrian camels, which live in Asia, have two humps." One boy summoned up a full complement of phonic and structural analysis skills and tried *Bakt-rin* and did blend these syllables into *Bakt rǝn?* While he blended the sounds, he shifted the second vowel sound to a schwa sound—not an unreasonable strategy. However, the questioning tone of his voice made it clear he was unsure about the accuracy of his pronunciation. He had no real word in his listening/speaking vocabulary with which to compare the product of his word attack.

While a discussion about camels prior to reading the selection in question will not reveal all the vocabulary a child knows about the topic, it will give a general impression which might provide the examiner with a helpful framework for interpreting the child's performance.

Many important diagnostic considerations with regard to decoding skills will be discussed in the next section. However, one important consideration an examiner must make is determining whether difficulty in word pronunciation (decoding) appears to be primarily a reflection of limited listening and speaking vocabulary. The readiness/purpose setting phase of an IRI can yield at least some information about the child's oral and aural vocabulary development.

Effect on comprehension. It is not enough to know that a child has a reading comprehension problem. To effectively correct that problem, it is critical to know something about why the problem exists. Several factors can significantly contribute to a comprehension problem; the remediation approach of choice will vary depending on the major source(s) of the problem. One major reason for children failing to comprehend the content of a selection is that they do not bring sufficient prior knowledge about the topic to their reading of the selection. The examiner can develop a framework for interpreting comprehension behavior by 1) giving children the title of the selection or the topic of a paragraph, 2) showing them accompanying illustrations, and 3) asking them to tell what they already know about the topic and what they think the selection might be about. Consider these rather extreme examples of responses from two different fourth grade children who were told they would be reading a few paragraphs about present day China. They were asked what they thought the paragraphs might tell about.

Child One: "I think China is someplace in Japan. I think the king of China was very mean and tried to make slaves of lots of people."

Child Two: "It might tell about the size of China. China is very large and has lots of people. It might also tell about government. The government of China is communist."

It would not be surprising if the first child had difficulty in understanding and remembering the content of an expository article about China. He appears to have limited information or even misinformation. Since the last part of the child's statement seems to reflect an anticipation of past, historical information, he didn't key in the information that the paragraph would give facts about "present day" China.

Though it is hardly a novel idea, the past five years of reading research have vividly pointed out that reading comprehension is a by-product of the interaction of what the reader brings to a selection and the information contained in that selection. How well a selection is understood and whether it is comprehended at all will depend on a reader's prior knowledge or background of experience. In the past decade, schema has been used to refer to the relevant background knowledge a reader brings to a text. The schema allows for an integration and interpretation of what the author wishes to convey through printed text.

Thus far the discussion of background knowledge has emphasized the effect of limited background. However, effectively using the readiness/purpose setting phase of an IRI also can lead to understanding another type of reader—the one who gives very reasonable, sometimes accurate answers to comprehension questions, but whose answers do not reflect awareness of the content contained in the selection just read. For example, in response to a selection dealing with feeding cats, one young girl gave full, articulate answers; however, she answered the questions almost exclusively on the basis of her prior knowledge. She took no notice of the advice the author of the selection offered about feeding cats. The examiner felt rather confident in concluding that this girl was overrelying on prior knowledge since what she said before reading the selection was clearly reflected in her answers to questions following the reading. Obviously, having such information will allow the examiner to make more specific, more accurate recommendations for improving this girl's comprehension abilities. Efficient reading of a text requires the active integration of text information with knowledge a reader already possesses. In the case of the girl just cited, there was insufficient attention to text information and overreliance on prior knowledge.

In addition to evaluating background knowledge, the prereading phase of an IRI can and should be used to evaluate a reader's ability to set purposes for reading. At times, especially for content area reading materials, it is appropriate for the examiner to give the student a purpose for reading the selection; however, much diagnostic information can be gathered if the examiner encourages the child to speculate on the possible content of a selection. For example, an illustration accompanying a primary level selection showed two adults and two children riding in a car with an airport in the background. Again, compare the responses of two different children when they were asked to look at the picture and tell what they thought the selection might be about.

Child One: "There's a man and a lady and a boy and a girl. There's an airplane."
(Examiner asks what might happen.)
"The airplane might land."
(Anything else?)
"It might take off."

Child Two: "It could be about how the mother and the kids were taking the father to the airport because he was going on a trip to Boston. He'll buy them some treats there for when he gets home."

Obviously, the predictions about the content reveal differences in background of experience. Notice, however, even in this brief response the first child reveals the possession of some important concepts about airports and planes. A significant difference seems to lie in the children's willingness to take a minimal amount of information from a picture and blend it with background of experience. Child One is very guarded and talks mainly about what is actually present in the picture. The predictions are safe—the plane shown hovering over the airport is said to be either landing or taking off. In contrast, Child Two is much freer, more spontaneous in her predictions. She uses the picture as a jumping off point to do exactly what the examiner suggested—speculate on what the selection "might be about." This information was extremely useful in interpreting the later comprehension performance of the children. Child Two's comprehension of materials read was excellent; Child One did very well with literal recall information but had great difficulty with questions requiring inferencing, expression of opinion, or critical evaluation.

Finally, the readiness/purpose setting phase affords an excellent opportunity to gain some impression of the interest and enthusiasm with which the reader approaches a selection. Learning from the prereading discussion whether a child loves, feels lukewarm about, or hates the subject discussed can be useful in interpreting a child's performance on a selection dealing with that subject.

Oral Reading Performance

After background of experience has been explored and purposes established for reading in an IRI, the child is asked to read aloud a paragraph of text material. This procedure is definitely undesirable for reading instruction since, under most natural circumstances, children and adults have an opportunity to read material silently before reading orally. In instructional settings, oral reading at sight may create unnecessary stress on a child. However, oral reading at sight seems justifiable for diagnostic purposes since it reveals as fully as possible the difficulties a child encounters when reading. For example, the illustration of the child working out the word *angry* (earlier in this chapter) provides useful information about how the child approaches decoding challenges. The child's responses indicated that responding to that word certainly was not a trouble free process. If the child had first read the selection silently, valuable diagnostic information might have been lost and an unrealistically positive impression of the child's decoding skills formed. Unquestionably, additional information is needed in order to more firmly ground the practice of using oral reading at sight, but lacking definitive information, we fall back upon experience and illustrations as bases of continuing the practice of using oral reading at sight as a diagnostic procedure. (For a more complete discussion of the factors surrounding the issue of oral versus silent reading processes see Leu, 1982.)

A child's ability to accurately and fluently read the sentences of a paragraph reflects many skills. The primary purposes for evaluating oral reading performance are to determine if decoding skills are being used in an efficient, integrated fashion; to determine if any weaknesses exist in major skill areas; and to look for clues which suggest that limitations in decoding are negatively affecting comprehension.

The previous section of this chapter discussed how word knowledge or vocabulary development might influence the decoding of a word. The prereading discussion might also yield valuable information about the syntactic development of a child. If the child has developed only restricted sentence patterns, calling for reading longer, more elaborate sentences might result in a very labored, nonfluent oral reading performance.

Chapter 3 presented a shorthand system for recording oral reading. After the completion of the IRI, the examiner will use that record to count errors in order to derive an oral-reading-in-context score and to diagnostically assess the nature of the miscues or errors made. A number of skill areas must be developed and integrated if a child is to achieve accurate, efficient reading. Following are major areas of consideration that can be evaluated from the record of a child's oral reading performance on an IRI.

Instant recognition vocabulary. This is also referred to as "sight" vocabulary. Mature readers only rarely stop to analyze or sound out words as they read. Individual words are recognized in a fraction of a second. It is especially important that high frequency words—those which occur repeatedly in print—be recognized instantly. If a child has to stop and try to figure out *the, of, and, a, to, in, is, you, that,* and *it*—the ten words a comprehensive study by Carroll, Davis, and Richman (1971) suggests appear most frequently in print—oral reading will be slow, labored, and expressionless. If children must focus so much of their attention on analyzing words such as the ten listed, it is almost certain they will not be able to attend to the message of the author, and comprehension will suffer. (See Barr, 1984; Lesgold & Resnick, 1982, for a discussion of the need for automaticity in decoding skills.) It is important to keep in mind how frequently and where hesitations occur during oral reading. It is also important to note that high frequency words often do not follow phonic generalizations and, therefore, need to be recognized through an approach other than phonic analysis.

Use of context clues. In one evaluation, a boy read a sentence as "Before going to bed I like to have a glass of milk and a doorknob." Without pausing, the child went on to read the next sentence. The last word actually printed in the sentence was *doughnut,* not *doorknob.* Given a stock of instantly recognized high frequency words, sampling *some* of the print in a word that is not immediately identifiable often results in accurate, rapid word recognition, if the knowledge of letter/sound association for the print is combined with context clues (using the meaning of other words in a sentence to help identify a specific word). The oral reading performance on an IRI should yield considerable information about the use of context clues. Children who read slowly, often in a word by word fashion, often have not learned to adequately use context clues. Children who substitute words that "don't make sense" in a sentence also are demonstrating deficiency in using this skill.

One indication of the effective use of context clues occurs when a child spontaneously corrects an error. If the child in the illustration used in the beginning of this section had been using the accumulated meaning in the sentence or paragraph (if other sentences related to food preceded this one) he would have known that *doorknob* didn't make sense. If this were the case, in all likelihood he would have stopped, looked more carefully at the letters in the word *doughnut,* and brought to mind relevant phonic and structural analysis skills. If all this was done while remembering the word was a food to be eaten along with drinking milk, the probability seems high that *doorknob* would have been corrected to *doughnut.* Good readers engage in "comprehension monitoring" as they read. They evaluate new information derived from their reading in light of what they already know (prior knowledge) and what they have already read in a selection. If something students read doesn't fit what would be expected, based on these two factors, they critically reevaluate the last information. One possible consequence of such behavior is the discovery of word recognition errors which are then corrected.

There is evidence (Kibby, 1979; Leslie & Osol, 1974; Williamson & Young, 1974) to suggest that the nature of the errors or miscues a reader makes depends on the level of challenge the material presents. For materials at an independent or instructional level, the reader has good instant recognition vocabulary and can use context clues. As materials become increasingly difficult, more words must be analyzed, context clues become less available, and reading becomes slow and labored. In most instances, comprehension suffers. Because strategies used by many readers are influenced by the level of difficulty, there is danger (when trying to do a qualitative analysis) in merging information from all levels of the IRI administered. Instead, a diagnostician should look at the interaction between the level of challenge and the reader strategies employed. The ability to use context clues and to correct errors made will suffer as a result of encountering materials at a reader's frustration level.

Keeping in mind the use and power of context clues will help an examiner put into proper perspective some word substitutions, omissions, or insertions readers sometimes make. Children who substitute *car* for *automobile, Dad* for *Father,* or *house* for *home* are reflecting their use of context clues. This leads to the need to address a point briefly mentioned in Chapter 2 – not all word recognition errors are equally "bad." Before defending and explaining that position, it seems important to review (in an abbreviated, oversimplified way) what probably happens during the process of oral reading for readers who are beyond the beginning stages of reading. It is important to note that children of any age who are at the beginning stages of learning to read probably process printed words in a less fluent, word by word manner than described here.

1. If prereading discussion took place, the reader begins reading a selection with certain expectations about the content of the selection and of the words

used to express that content. If the prereading discussion centered around airports, *planes, landing, take-off, ticket counter,* and *baggage* are words for which the reader has a mental set. Words like *tadpole, lily pad, croak,* and *forked tongue* are not expected; they go with an anticipation of reading about frogs.

2. If the selection is at the readers' independent or instructional levels, it seems likely they will instantly recognize many of the words in the first sentence. Therefore, sentence context clues are brought into play.

3. Just enough graphic (print) clues are focused on to help confirm or deny what readers expect to find on the page, based on prior knowledge, expectations, and previous reading.

4. At an independent or instructional level, the readers' eyes will focus on words ahead of those being orally pronounced. This is sometimes referred to as the eye-voice span. Looking ahead of words being read orally allows for better oral expression and more adequate use of context clues.

5. Since there is distance between pronouncing words and visually taking in words, it seems likely the information picked up visually is briefly stored in the reader's memory.

6. The words fluent readers are pronouncing, then, are based on what is stored in memory rather than on the words visually seen.

The six steps listed are certainly not meant to be a description of the total reading process, just a partial description of what is involved in fluent oral reading. However, if this description is accepted, it becomes easier to see why substitutions of words like *house* for *home* or *car* for *auto* can occur. The form in which the processed print is stored will be the syntactic and semantic form most familiar to the reader. When the reader's eyes hit the word *home,* and if reading for meaning is the object, it is possible that *a place to live* is what really gets stored in memory. When it is time to read, the stored memory may be pronounced (orally read) as *house* since that is the word the reader uses to refer to a place to live. Given the proposed description of the oral reading process, it would not seem startling that the printed sentence, "He sits quietly waiting for the principal." is read as "He is sitting quietly and waiting for the principal." The way the sentence was read may simply reflect syntactic forms more commonly used by the reader.

Given the description of how oral reading may take place, it is obvious we are engaging in gross oversimplification and potential distortion if we weigh the substitution of *doorknob* for *doughnut* as equal or less than the substitution of *is sitting* for *sits.* To our knowledge, no one has been able to propose a quantitative system for weighing oral reading errors that has received either experimental verification or widespread acceptance. Since this is the case, we continue to recommend the counting of errors as suggested in Chapter 3, followed by a qualitative interpretation of the nature and gravity of the errors made. The best touchstone for the qualitative interpretation of errors is the extent to which they distort the message of the text. The Appendix offers illustrations of such qualitative interpretations.

Before summarizing some of the important questions a diagnostician needs to address with respect to an oral reading performance, two additional issues need to be mentioned: the use of *error* versus *miscue* and the influence of dialect speech on oral reading performance.

The term *miscue* was introduced in Chapter 1. We agree there are likely to be reasons why, in oral reading, a reader says something different from what is printed in the text being read. In this sense, *miscue* seems preferable, if the connotation of the word *error* is that the departure from print is random. Our concern is that some users of *miscue* fail to recognize that deviations are indications of reading difficulties and may detract from getting the meaning of a selection or else reflect inefficient approaches to decoding. If the option seemed realistically available, we would reserve *miscue* for oral reading deviations from print that did very little to alter the meaning of the text, and reserve *error* for those deviations that did change meaning. It seems unlikely, at this time, that such a proposal would achieve widespread acceptance.

The American Heritage Dictionary defines dialect as: "A regional variety of language, distinguished from other varieties by pronunciation, grammar, or vocabulary." While different from standard forms, dialect speech is just as systematic but, as the definition indicates, it is different in "pronunciation, grammar, or vocabulary." If a reader has achieved some degree of reading fluency and is operating as described previously in this chapter, the oral reading will probably reflect the reader's dialect speech since the reader's representation of the meaning derived from the print is what will be pronounced. For example, if the reader lived in a part of the country where the word *pen* is pronounced with a short *i,* is it surprising that he or she would pronounce it as *pin* or *pi-en*? Likewise, a child whose syntax does not require a linking verb in sentences like: "She is my mother." is likely to orally read that sentence as "She my mother." If a child is a fluent reader, we expect oral reading to reflect the speech characteristics the child has developed. A standard reading of the text will develop as the child develops greater mastery of standard speech. To expect a child to do standard reading of a text before developing standard speech is to ask the child to abandon fluent, more meaning oriented reading strategies and to resort to beginning, word by word or even letter by letter reading strategies. If the examiner has a reasonable basis for judging that a child read something different from what was printed, but the difference was a reflection of the child's dialect, we recommend *against* counting those deviations when calculating an oral reading percentage score. It would be appropriate in the qualitative interpretations for the examiner to indicate the extent and nature of the dialect differences. The topic of dialect as it relates to reading is complex, controversial, and emotionally charged.

To review and slightly extend the considerations that should go into qualitatively interpreting the oral reading performance on an IRI, it is recommended an examiner use the following list of questions.

- Does the oral reading performance of the child reflect a balanced use of instant recognition vocabulary, context clues, phonics skills, and structural analysis skills? Do weaknesses appear to exist in any of these skill areas?
- Is the child reading in a hesitant, word by word fashion or does the child seem to have achieved some degree of fluency in oral reading?
- Do vocabulary or concept limitations appear to be adversely affecting oral reading performance?
- How serious were the errors or miscues the reader made? To what extent did they interfere with or alter the meaning of the selection being read?
- Does the reader appear to be reading for meaning, engaging in comprehension monitoring, and correcting oral reading errors that adversely affect meaning?
- To what extent is oral reading performance a reflection of the child's dialect?

Assessing reading comprehension. Chapter 3 indicated that the procedures used for assessing the comprehension of orally read materials are virtually the same as those used for assessing silently read materials. Therefore, the bulk of this chapter will focus on the common interpretation that can be made for both types of comprehension checks.

The discussion of estimating reading levels in Chapter 2 offered some guidelines for interpreting the amount of comprehension expected. Unless readers can successfully respond to about 75 percent of the questions posed about a selection read, it seems unlikely they will be successful in mastering the content of that material, even with teacher guidance. The next question diagnosticians would like to ask is, "What specific comprehension skills are well or poorly developed for this reader?" Unfortunately, this latter type of interpretation is extremely difficult since there is no definitive, agreed upon list of reading comprehension skills. While it would please most diagnosticians to be able to make statements about a reader's skills areas such as main idea, drawing conclusions, predicting outcomes, cause and effect relationships, and summarizing, we cannot find good evidence to suggest that such specifically designated skills areas can be accurately and separately diagnosed. For this reason we suggested in Chapter 2 that IRI questions be classified more broadly as vocabulary, factual, inferential, and evaluative. We immediately acknowledge that even such broad differentiations are not supported by research as capable of being separately assessed. Nevertheless, it seems useful to ask if one of these four broad types seems to be a particular problem area. This permits at least some diagnosis of the overall IRI performance beyond just indicating that a problem exists in reading comprehension. It also seems important to point out that if IRI users feel they can specifically assess skills areas, the informal, flexible nature of the IRI allows for the writing, inclusion, and interpretation of such questions.

Qualitative interpretations for the comprehension of a portion of an IRI also require looking at the pattern of scores. Consider, for example, one child's comprehension scores at third, fourth, and fifth reader levels.

Level	Oral Comprehension	Silent Comprehension	Average Comprehension
Third	80	85	83
Fourth	65	60	63
Fifth	75	85	80

The numerical criterion (75 percent) for an instructional level performance is clearly met by this child's performance at third and fifth levels, but not fourth. An immediate question would be whether the performance is artificially low at fourth or spuriously high at fifth. In many cases, the content of the selection will strongly influence comprehension. Here the importance of information gathered in the prereading readiness activities is once again accented. Did the child demonstrate a weak background of experience for or a lack of interest in the content of the fourth reader selection, or an unusually well developed background for or interest in the fifth reader selection? Could other factors have influenced the performance?

Actually, the examiner's final conclusion for this child was that the selections through third reader level were all narrative, story type materials but that at fourth they shifted to being fact oriented, expository selections. The child's behavior and comments indicated she was not accustomed to reading such materials; however, as a result of her experience with just the two fourth grade selections, her performance was considerably improved at fifth reader level. Her difficulty and her quick recovery have clear diagnostic significance. Justification for establishing her instructional level at fifth was supported by the fact that her oral reading comprehension score at sixth (which is not listed in the summary shown) was 60 and her silent reading score was 65 — essentially the same numerical scores she achieved at fourth grade level. The fact that her performance did not seriously deteriorate at sixth was very encouraging.

Substantial and consistent differences between oral and silent reading performance required interpretation. For example, one bright sixth grade boy achieved the following comprehension scores on an IRI.

Level	Oral Comprehension	Silent Comprehension	Average Comprehension
Sixth	55	85	70
Seventh	50	90	70
Eighth	45	80	63

According to the strict numerical criterion, this youngster, whose records indicated that he does very well in school performance including reading, falls slightly below an instructional level even at sixth grade. Notice, however, that the scores in silent comprehension are consistently above the 75 percent criterion. Since we would expect that most of the important reading activities this sixth grader engages in would be completed silently, we have a tendency to attach more importance to this form of comprehension performance. We previously acknowledged that oral reading at sight has some limitations when trying to evaluate overall reading performance. In the case of this student, the examiner took one additional step. Because of the apparent maturity of the reader, the examiner told him his comprehension was consistently better when he read silently as compared to when he read orally. The student replied that he wasn't surprised; he always felt uncomfortable when he had to read aloud because he feared he would make mistakes. Given the combination of anxiety and a focus of attention on word pronunciation, it hardly seems surprising that comprehension suffered. Interestingly, this boy was able to read orally sixth through eighth reader materials nearly perfectly, with a minimum of 98 percent word recognition accuracy. This situation also indicates the diagnostic value of a careful examiner question.

While the focus of the previous discussion was a difference between oral and silent reading, it also served to introduce the next area of qualitative interpretation of comprehension — trying to determine the factor(s) which may be contributing to the breakdown in comprehension. In the illustration just reviewed, factors such as attention and affect (in this case, attitudes about oral reading) appeared to have an adverse effect on comprehension of orally read materials. Information gathered during prereading discussion and observance of the child's behavior during the evaluation frequently yield valuable information about general attitudes toward reading, attitudes toward a particular topic of reading, and the ability to focus attention and concentration.

Some comprehension problems are the direct result of limitations in decoding skills. Certainly, one can expect comprehension to suffer as the word recognition in context score drops below 95 percent accuracy. However, it is also quite possible for a reader to maintain "accurate" oral reading while limitations in decoding serve as a major contributor to a comprehension problem. For example, children who have failed to develop the ability to instantly recognize high frequency words or who rarely use context clues will need to focus their attention on analyzing words rather than on interpreting the message of the author. Such reading is often marked by numerous hesitations and, while in a sense the oral reading is accurate, it is labored and inefficient.

An excellent way to make diagnostic interpretations about the role of decoding skills in comprehension is to compare reading comprehension performance with listening comprehension performance. One of the most obvious differences between reading and listening comprehension is that in listening, the child does not have to visually decode. Cognitive processes and vocabulary or other linguistic demands for listening and reading comprehension are strikingly similar. If a child performs well in listening comprehension but poorly in reading comprehension, limitations or inefficiencies in decoding probably exist; nevertheless, there are other explanations for the disparate performance.

Another, often overlooked, source of reading comprehension difficulties is the reader's failure to adequately use graphic and punctuation cues. Children with this limitation often perform well on listening comprehension tests where the person reading to them uses appropriate pauses and intonation to aid comprehension. However, children encounter difficulty when they must use italics, boldface print, parentheses, headings, and punctuation marks as aids to comprehension. The quality of children's oral reading performance will often serve as a good basis for diagnosing difficulties in interpreting punctuation and other graphic aids.

We have touched on the critical role of vocabulary, concept development, and background knowledge in this chapter and in other sections of this book. When failures in comprehension occur, it is necessary for the diagnostician to review the results of the prereading readiness discussion. Comparison of listening and reading comprehension performance once again will be helpful. If background knowledge is generally weak, both reading and listening comprehension are likely to be deficient.

Much of what has been said about qualitative interpretation of a child's comprehension performance on an IRI applies to both questioning and retelling strategies; however, some special considerations apply to interpreting retellings. Retellings offer another opportunity for the diagnostician to evaluate the language development of the child. Retellings are less structured than questioning strategies and children may reveal a wide range of sentence patterns and vocabulary usage. With retellings it is informative to review the volume of ideas reflected in the child's retelling. How much more information was the child able to report when questioning probes were used? What kind of information did the child include in the retellings—main idea, important information, details, or a mixture of these? One should expect important information from a selection to be included in the retellings.

Another important consideration is the extent to which information is organized in the retellings. Does it reflect the structures used in the text read? If the text was structured around comparisons and contrasts, was the retelling similarly organized? Did the reader impose some different organization, or was the retelling more like a random collection of facts? Finally, retellings should be analyzed for the extent to which they include information not contained in the materials read. Not all such elaborations or intrusions are bad; some demonstrate active thinking, inferencing on the part of the reader. The Appendix offers some illustrations of these.

One last point: Whether using a questioning strategy, a retelling strategy, or a combination of both for assessing comprehension, what is being measured is *memory* for what was comprehended. In many cases, the failure to perform well on the comprehension measure is the result of a failure to remember. On the other hand, there are readers whose backgrounds of experience, language development, or decoding skills are so limited that the material was never understood in the first place. Separating the understanding from the memory aspects for reading comprehension is fairly simple; after the completion of a more formal aspect of comprehension evaluation, allow the child to refer to the text to answer questions missed or to elaborate on an incomplete retelling. (See Appendix for an illustration of how this can be done efficiently.)

Assessing listening comprehension. Gaining information about the level at which students can listen to and understand material read to them is a useful area of evaluation. Many of the interpretive considerations that apply to reading comprehension also apply to listening comprehension. Some examples are interpretation of the type of comprehension problems that exist; the influence of interest, attention, and background of experience; the type of information included in retellings; and the organization of retellings. It is essential to recognize that the basic language and conceptual skills underlying listening and reading comprehension are similar. The preceding discussion of reading comprehension showed how valuable diagnostic interpretations can be made by contrasting listening and reading comprehension performances. Proximity of the listening and reading comprehension levels indicates that the development of decoding skills is sufficient to allow readers to use reading to exercise the language skills developed. Further growth in reading requires further growth in language and concept development. Many disabled readers who are having difficulty in acquiring decoding skills can often perform at a much higher level in listening comprehension than reading comprehension. The language base is there upon which to build. Remember that children in the beginning stages of reading, whether very young or seriously disabled readers, have been developing language skills for five or six years (more in the case of disabled readers) and expect their listening comprehension to be higher than their reading comprehension. By about third reader level, one sees a convergence of the reading and listening comprehension levels which continues through subsequent years. By junior or high school levels, many readers perform better in reading than in listening. An efficient reader can use reading more effectively than listening – slowing down at difficult points, reading faster at easy points, and rereading as necessary. Listening usually does not afford the same flexibility as reading does for the skilled reader.

Oral rereading performance. A variety of reading functions can be qualitatively evaluated through having a child reread aloud selections previously read silently.

Under most practical circumstances, students first read silently the material they are to read aloud. It does not make sense that anyone would want to read something of unknown content to someone else. Therefore, it is interesting and diagnostically useful to compare readers' oral reading at sight performance with their oral rereading of materials previously read silently. One should expect oral rereading to be of better quality; however, children with severe reading problems often show no improvement in oral rereading compared to oral reading at sight.

Oral rereading is an excellent way to form impressions of a child's flexibility in rate of reading. As noted earlier, the procedures for oral rereading required the child to locate and read aloud from the passage the answer to a question posed by the examiner. Some children demonstrate excellent ability to rapidly skim the previously read section and efficiently locate the information requested. Inefficient readers, however, begin careful rereading at the beginning of the selection and proceed at a rate and in a fashion similar to their original silent reading. The latter performance obviously suggests a need for instruction in flexibility in rate of reading.

The oral rereading function also affords an opportunity to assess the youngster's ability to read for a specific purpose and to locate specific information. In response to oral rereading questions, some children read irrelevant information or much more information than needed to answer the examiner's questions. Such responses serve as a basis for concluding that the child's difficulty lies with basic interpretation of the information rather than with just remembering the information.

Oral rereading can be helpful in allowing a diagnostician to separate problems in understanding text material from problems in remembering text material. After a comprehension check is completed, it is helpful to have children return to the passage previously read and try to locate the information they were unable to produce for the examiner's questions. Obviously, if a child can locate and read the correct information, memory, not basic understanding, appears to be the problem.

Concluding Statements

IRIs are commonly used to establish reading levels. Chapter 2 outlined the criteria applied for the establishment of those levels. This chapter, which should be used along with the case illustrations in the Appendix, serves as a basis for integrating qualitative information so levels are established with greater precision and as a basis for better understanding the nature of a reader's approach to the complex activity called reading. Prereading discussion, oral reading performance, comprehension assessment, and oral rereading performance are all rich sources of diagnostic information. With experience in the administration and interpretation of IRIs and with varying purposes for using IRIs, many additional interpretations will be possible.

Chapter 5
Individual Word Recognition Tests

Individual word recognition tests represent another aspect of informal reading evaluation. While word recognition tests are not an integral part of an IRI, they are commonly used with IRIs. The term *word recognition test* as used in this booklet (and in other publications dealing with the evaluation of reading skills), refers to a measure of a child's ability to recognize words in isolation; that is, words that do not appear in the context of a sentence or longer text. It is appropriate to think of IRIs and word recognition tests as interwoven. However, there is a strong tendency for those just becoming familiar with the use of IRIs to confuse the oral reading context score from an inventory with the score from a word recognition test and to sometimes inappropriately use the results of word recognition tests to estimate reading levels. Therefore, we decided to treat word recognition tests in this separate chapter, hoping for greater clarity.

Nature and Purpose of Individual Word Recognition Tests

As noted, in a word recognition test the subject is asked to identify isolated words—words that are isolated from the natural context of a sentence. In this sense, a word recognition test is somewhat artificial; it denies the reader the use of one of the most potent means of word recognition—sentence context. It does, however, give the examiner an opportunity to focus more specifically on children's ability to immediately recognize word forms (sometimes called sight vocabulary or instant recognition vocabulary), as well as ability to analyze phonic and structural aspects of words they cannot immediately identify (sometimes called word analysis or word attack skills). Word recognition tests also can be used to provide an *estimate* of the level at which to begin administering an IRI.

Words for a word recognition list are best chosen from materials available (or being considered) for use in instruction. It is recommended that twenty-five words be chosen from each level of difficulty of the material. Thus, if a basal reader program is used in a school, a separate word recognition list of twenty-five words can be constructed for each level of that series, preprimer through sixth or eighth level. Basal readers and instructional materials designed for use in corrective or remedial programs introduced at a particular level of difficulty include lists of words that did not appear at an earlier level. By randomly selecting only from these "new words," the examiner can be assured the lists will become progressively more challenging from level to level. When words are chosen in the manner recommended, the graded lists of words should be reasonable samples of the word recognition skills required by the instructional materials from which they were taken. Caution should be used in generalizing the results to other instructional materials, since reading vocabulary demands and the skills required for word recognition vary from one set of materials to another.

The words in word recognition tests are usually presented in list form. For actual test material, these lists of words should be in clear, readable type to avoid the possibility of resulting recognition difficulty reflecting the vagueness or distortion of the visual stimulus, rather than the child's inability to recognize words in the test. More detailed directions for constructing word recognition tests are included in Chapter 6. The purpose of this chapter is to provide an overview of word recognition lists, how they are administered, and the major interpretations drawn from them.

Administration of Informal Word Recognition Tests

The method for administering an informal word recognition test is dictated by the main purpose of this instrument—to obtain an indication of the child's sight vocabulary and word analysis skills. If one wants to measure instantaneous recognition of words, controlling the time such words are exposed is of primary importance. Thus, words on this test are first exposed in a timed (rapid) or tachistoscopic (time controlled) presentation. The manual technique for rapidly exposing the words to the child is relatively simple but requires practice to be executed smoothly. The materials needed are 3 x 5 index cards, a word list from which the child will read, and a record form for the examiner. Seated next to the child, the examiner places the word list directly in front of the child with the recording form placed to the examiner's side. To rapidly present a word to the child, the two cards are held together immediately above the first word on the list. The lower card is moved down to expose the word; the upper card is then moved down to close the opening between them. This complete series of motions is carried out quickly, giving the child only a brief presentation of the word. It is important, however, that the word be exposed completely and clearly. A tendency in inexperienced examiners is to follow the lower card with the upper one, thus never really giving a clear exposure of the word. If a child responds correctly to the timed presentation, the examiner continues to repeat the same procedure with the next word as long as there is immediate recognition of the words. Keep in mind that the time during which a word is exposed must be carefully controlled. The examiner may move from one word to the next at a pace comfortable for both the examiner and the child being tested.

If the word is exposed, the cards closed, and the child gives an incorrect response or fails to respond in approximately a second, the word is reexposed by moving the upper card so the word can be seen. The cards are left open so the child can further examine the exposed word. This portion of the administration is referred to as the "untimed exposure," since the child has as much time as is needed to apply word analysis skills to identify the word. No clues are given by the examiner, but the child has the opportunity to reexamine the word and to apply whatever word analysis skills the child has developed. While the child is attempting to work out the pronunciation of a word, the examiner should record (on the recording copy) the incorrect response given by the child, following the timed exposure.

After the child makes a response during the untimed exposure, or it is judged the child will not be able to identify a word, the examiner returns to the timed exposure presentation of the remaining words until, once again, one word is not immediately identified correctly or is misidentified. During the untimed exposure of the word, the examiner should encourage the child to make some response. Unless a fairly sizable number of responses are obtained, the potential for making diagnostic interpretations of areas of strength and weakness in word analysis will be limited. All responses, timed and untimed, should be recorded.

When several grade or reader levels of word lists are used as a word recognition test, the examiner may wish to estimate the level at which testing should be initiated. Any available information about the child's present or past reading performance may be helpful. The goal is to obtain a relatively perfect performance on the lowest level list employed. If weaknesses are detected at the beginning level of the word recognition test, the examiner should return to an easier list before testing with a more difficult one. In the absence of any information about a child, is is best to start with the easiest level of the word recognition test. If the list is too easy, the child will move through it in a matter of minutes and very little time will be lost. In such cases, some examiners abbreviate testing at the easy levels by presenting only half of the words and quickly moving to the next level.

The word recognition test is continued, moving from level to level, until the child is no longer able to perform adequately at any given level. Unless the situation is extremely frustrating, it is advisable to continue the test until the child is able to recognize, in the untimed exposure, 25 percent or fewer of the words in the list at the level being administered.

Flexibility is required in administering an individual word recognition list. While it is helpful to continue administering the untimed portion of the test until few words are recognized, little diagnostically useful information is gained by continuing the timed presentation beyond the point where less than 50 percent of the words are recognized. When this rate is reached, discontinue the timed procedure and have the child attempt to pronounce each of the remaining words on the list at his or her own rate.

Recording Performance on Informal Word Recognition Tests

The following shorthand system is recommended for recording responses on this instrument for both timed and untimed responses.

$\checkmark$ = correct response

o = no response

dk = a statement from the child that he or she does not know the word

y-e-s = separated letters indicate a naming of letters

There is no simple shorthand for recording incorrect responses made by the child. Responses need to be recorded as completely and accurately as possible. This is quite easy when one word is substituted for another. For example, if the word on the list was *boy* and the child said *bug,* the examiner would record *bug* in the appropriate blank on the recording sheet. Some children will give responses that are not real words; here, the examiner should record the child's response as phonetically as possible. The object is to later be able to tell exactly what the child said in response to the word. Using diacritical marking for long vowel sounds (e.g. bōggle) and short vowel sounds (e.g. lăker) is frequently helpful.

Recording sheets should be prepared with the word to the left followed by a line on which to record the timed response and a space, and then another line on which to record the untimed response. Immediate responses are recorded in the timed response column. The responses for reexposures of the word appear in the untimed column. If a word is instantly recognized, a $\checkmark$will appear in the timed column with nothing in the untimed column.

It is important for responses to be recorded immediately, so there is complete accuracy in the record of the performance. Even a few seconds delay in writing down the child's response may lead to confusion and incorrect reporting on the part of the examiner. Here, also, the use of a tape recorder is helpful.

Scoring Word Recognition Lists

Two scores will be derived from each list of words; one representing immediate recognition of the words (timed presentation) and the other, total recognition of words at this level when given the time needed to decode the words (untimed presentation). In each case, the percentage of words correct is the final score. On the timed test, only correct responses given immediately are counted in the basic score. If corrections are made spontaneously without a reexposure of the word, credit is given for independent correction, but the basic percentage score does not change. Thus, on a list of twenty words, if a child pronounced nineteen correctly and one wrong, the basic score for immediate recognition of words (timed section) would be 95 percent; if the child made an immediate correction of the twentieth word without seeing it again, a +1 should be added to the record of the scoring. The 95 percent +1 would indicate that the one error had been corrected without teacher aid.

The percentage score for the untimed column consists of all the words correctly identified instantly, plus all the words correctly identified in the untimed exposure; in the situation just cited, a score of 100 percent.

There are two final percentage scores derived from a word recognition test; one reflecting instant recognition of words and the other representing ability to recognize words without time restrictions. These two scores are not combined or averaged.

The following example shows two levels of one boy's word recognition test as his responses were recorded. Where an incorrect response was recorded and followed by a check, Robert made a spontaneous correction. A zero preceding a word or a checkmark indicates an unusual delay before responding.

The 75 + 1 percent score at preprimer level indicates that Robert initially read correctly fifteen of the twenty words during the timed presentation, and the + 1 notation indicates that he made one spontaneous correction without seeing the word again. His 80 percent untimed score represents credit for only the sixteen words which were recognized instantly, because Robert made no additional corrections during the untimed presentation. At primer level, however, he immediately correctly recognized only eight words; two additional words were recognized with some hesitation, but before the examiner showed them for an extended period of time, thus Robert's immediate recognition score was 32 + 2. When given unlimited time, Robert was able to decode three more words, which gave him an untimed score of 52 percent.

Word Recognition Test

Name _____Robert_____ Age __9__ Date _1/15/86_

Preprimer Level

	Stimulus	Timed	Untimed
1.	Little	✓	
2.	you	✓	
3.	can	✓	
4.	Play	✓	
5.	said	0	*something*
6.	Want	0	0
7.	come	✓	
8.	it	✓	
9.	comes	*came*	0
10.	Come	✓	
11.	for	✓	
12.	see	✓	
13.	play	✓	
14.	It	✓	
15.	I	✓	
16.	to	✓	
17.	in	*m* → ✓	
18.	Big	✓	
19.	not	*down*	0
20.	big	✓	
		75 + 1	80%

Primer Level

	Stimulus	Timed	Untimed
1.	Good	*oh- oh-dog*	*o*
2.	Run	✓	
3.	are	*can*	*and*
4.	like	*little*	*o*
5.	one	✓	
6.	Away	*never say the word*	*o*
7.	All	*o*	*dk*
8.	duck	*o*	*b-b-b-/o*
9.	yes	*y-e-s* ✓	
10.	get	*o*	*o*
11.	She	*her*	✓
12.	make	*o*	*m-m/o*
13.	my	✓	
14.	No	*oh, oh,* ✓	
15.	This	*o*	*they*
16.	am	*it, at*	*o*
17.	red	✓	
18.	run	✓	
19.	Do	✓	
20.	he	*d. remember*	*o*
21.	yellow	✓	
22.	Will	*what*	✓
23.	home	✓	
24.	went	*o*	*o*
25.	they	*o*	*came* ✓
		32+2	52%

Interpreting Results of Individual Word Recognition Tests

The use of word recognition lists allows an examiner to focus more specifically on phonic and structural analysis skills than is normally possible with oral reading activities that are part of IRIs. When a child is reading sentences and paragraphs, the effect of context can lead to the correct identification of a word a child might not be able to identify if it appeared without sentence context. It is important to know about a child's use of phonic and structural analysis skills since these are necessary word identification skills that need to be used in conjunction with language context skills. Context clues help narrow the choices for what a word might be, but rarely narrow the choices to a specific word. For example, the context, "My favorite fruit is _____." narrows the choices considerably. Syntactic clues narrow the choice to a noun or noun marker, while semantic clues indicate that the missing one names a fruit. However, graphic clues are necessary to tell which specific fruit. Nevertheless, while word recognition lists can be useful, asking a child to recognize an isolated word is not the typical task in reading. Rarely are children (or adults) called upon to perform such a task. Even words such as *EXIT* or *WALK* occur within a specific environmental context which aids in the recognition.

It might be useful to look at the results of a word recognition test and the potential interpretations that can be drawn from such a test. The results reported here are for Jeff, whose IRI results were reported in Chapter 3 of this book. Jeff's record of performance for lists ranging from preprimer to third reader level are reproduced here and are followed by a summary of his scores. The results of the word recognition list are discussed as if Jeff's IRI performance were not known, but the last section of this chapter makes a brief comparison of decoding skills from Jeff's IRI and word recognition tests.

Word Recognition Test

Name _____*Jeff*_____ Age _____ Date *1/26/86*

Preprimer Level

	Stimulus	Timed	Untimed
1.	we	✓	
2.	little	0	*lit* ✓
3.	was	✓	
4.	have	✓	
5.	with	✓	
6.	her	✓	
7.	said	✓	
8.	work	✓	
9.	cars	✓	
10.	ride	✓	
11.	see	✓	
12.	I	✓	
13.	is	✓	
14.	you	✓	
15.	a	✓	
16.	likes	✓	
17.	come	✓	
18.	in	✓	
19.	pet	0	✓
20.	and	✓	

Percent Correct ___90___ ___100___

Primer Level

	Stimulus	Timed	Untimed
1.	will	✓	
2.	she	✓	
3.	my	✓	
4.	put	✓	
5.	away	✓	
6.	baby	0	*boy*
7.	turnip	0	*tur-turning*
8.	went	✓	
9.	at	✓	
10.	ball	✓	
11.	want	✓	
12.	good	✓	
13.	read	✓	
14.	looked	*look*	✓
15.	he	✓	
16.	man	✓	
17.	what	*went*	*wăt* ✓
18.	take	✓	
19.	did	✓	
20.	ran	✓	
21.	black	0	*back*
22.	away	✓	
23.	will	✓	
24.	friend	0	*from*
25.	yellow	✓	

Percent Correct ___76___ ___84___

First Reader Level

	Stimulus	Timed	Untimed
1.	all	✓	
2.	they	✓	
3.	bus	✓	
4.	sat	✓	
5.	first	f-f-o	dk-fence
6.	grain		girls
7.	garden	o	gar-guard
8.	box	✓	
9.	your	✓	
10.	hot	✓	
11.	some	✓	
12.	wish	wash	wash
13.	but	✓	
14.	magic	misty	mighty
15.	there	✓	
16.	bread	bed	bird
17.	night	✓	
18.	lives	live	✓
19.	fish	✓	
20.	over	out	our
21.	smiled	o	✓
22.	lunch	o	✓
23.	library	o	dk - I really don't know
24.	stood	o	stoned
25.	happy	o	✓

Percent Correct   48   64

Second Reader Level

	Stimulus	Timed	Untimed
1.	plow		*poll* ✓
2.	room		✓
3.	everybody		o / dk *I never saw it*
4.	horns		
5.	sell		*steak*
6.	been		dk
7.	flew		dk
8.	please		dk
9.	strong		dk
10.	head		dk

not administered

10%

Administration discontinued at this point.

A number of dimensions are used to interpret the results of individual word recognition tests. Some of these are discussed here and Jeff's results are used to illustrate the kinds of conclusions that may be drawn.

Before that discussion it might be useful to gain an overall impression of Jeff's performance by looking at a summary of his scores on this test.

Level	% Timed	% Untimed
Preprimer	90	100
Primer	76	84
First	48	64
Second	–	10

Instant recognition vocabulary. Instant recognition or sight vocabulary refers to the stock of words a child can recognize immediately. Jeff immediately recognized almost all of the words in the preprimer list. His timed score of 90 percent represents a good performance; his ability to instantly recognize the words in a primer list is not as good. At primer level, Jeff can immediately recognize only about three-quarters of the words, suggesting that he will not recognize some of the vocabulary. The difficulties become more evident with first reader lists, and so widespread at second reader level that the examiner didn't even attempt to conduct a timed presentation of the words and discontinued the testing after the first ten words.

Word analysis skills. Jeff can bring word attack skills into play to successfully identify some words he cannot instantly recognize. If one compares his percentage scores for the timed and untimed columns at primer and first reader levels, there is improvement.

Jeff did not seem to analyze words in a letter by letter fashion. In many cases, he seemed to attend to the initial consonant element and then to almost guess at the remainder of the word. Frequently he represented the initial consonant correctly, but the middle and final portions of the word were incorrect, though final parts of the word were less likely to be incorrect than were middle portions. When Jeff misidentified a word, his response was always a real word; in no case did he respond with a nonsense word. This suggests that he is concerned with meaning but is insufficiently attentive to the graphic information in words. Vowel sounds seem particularly troublesome for Jeff, even in words where there is conformity to a phonic generalization (e.g., *wish*). He is also inconsistent in representing consonant clusters or blends. For example, Jeff correctly identifies *st* in *stood* and *fr* in *from* but incorrectly represents *bl* in *black*, *gr* in *grain*, *br* in *break*, and *pl* in *plow*. There was enough inconsistency in dealing with these fundamental word recognition elements to warrant review in this area.

Jeff's Test Performances Compared

Jeff is very consistent in his performance on the IRI and word recognition tests. Results from both suggest only mild difficulties at primer level, with more substantial difficulties at first reader level. At first reader level his difficulties in reading words in context are less dramatic than when reading isolated words. The comparison at this level suggests that Jeff is using context clues to aid in word identification. Test results suggest that he is trying to make sense of what he reads and is using strategies which seem to reflect dealing with reading as language.

Both sets of results also suggest strengths in the use of consonant letter-sound associations with attention focused on the initial part of the word. Jeff sometimes seems able to break words into parts but more commonly seems to guess at the decoding of a word based on initial consonant clues. This tendency is more apparent when he is asked to identify words in isolation.

Concluding Statements

Individual word recognition lists are another form of informal evaluation; they allow an examiner to obtain additional information about children's ability to immediately recognize words and to focus on skills used to analyze words not in their instant recognition vocabulary. Results from word recognition lists may be particularly useful when interpreted in light of the IRI results. Using scores from word recognition lists alone can lead to unreliable estimates about a child's overall reading capabilities. Performances on such lists, which involve identifying isolated words without use of context, are rather artificial. However, these results provide the diagnostician with useful information about the readers' use of phonic and other decoding skills. Further, they provide quick and useful estimates of starting levels for administration of an IRI.

Chapter 6
Constructing Informal Reading Inventories and Word Recognition Tests

One of the clearest potential advantages of IRIs for evaluating reading is the close match between materials used for testing and materials being considered for use in instruction. One widespread problem in the testing of reading is the measurement unit most frequently employed—reader or grade level, both terms being imprecise. For example, parameters of what constitutes second reader level material cannot be specified fully or with much precision. Even with minimal experience, it becomes obvious that not all books labeled as second reader level are equal in the skills they require or the degree of challenge they present. Therefore, using one set of test materials labeled as second reader level to generalize to a different set of instructional materials (even though they are labeled second reader level) is always somewhat questionable. In their simplest form, IRIs suggest the best way to determine if students can read a book is to sample their ability to read a portion of that book. By constructing an IRI, the teacher can accomplish this close match between diagnostic and instructional materials. It should be pointed out, however, that even this procedure of sampling from potential instructional materials is not totally free of drawbacks.

One potential problem in teacher constructed IRIs is that even reading materials "controlled" for difficulty will not be perfectly uniform in the challenge they present. While an entire book may be labeled second reader level, not all selections will be equally difficult; there may be variations in level of challenge from page to page of a given selection. Such variations are reasonable and to be expected in a reading text and can be effectively dealt with by providing varying amounts and different types of instruction. Such variations are bothersome, however, when the goal is to construct diagnostic materials which will allow conclusions to be drawn about a student's ability to deal with the entire text. The goal of the examiner constructing an IRI is to select passages representative of most of the material included at a given book level.

A second reason for recommending teacher constructed IRIs is that they bring about a greater level of teacher awareness of the process of evaluating reading. In constructing an IRI, a teacher is forced to analyze the material in more detailed, analytical, and critical ways. The teacher may be forced to try to formulate a reasonable set of comprehension questions, ones which tap a range of comprehension skills. By working through these procedures in constructing the inventory, the teacher will become more attuned to the way reading materials can be continuously used to gather diagnostic information during instructional periods. Finally, since almost any selection can be analyzed and found to require a wide variety of skills, the teacher can ask the kind of comprehension questions which will emphasize and actively tap skills considered to be most important in the reading curriculum of that teacher. The teacher who plans to emphasize use of topic sentences and derivation of main ideas as focal skills when working with fifth reader level materials can emphasize such skills when constructing the IRI.

Selecting Materials for Informal Reading Inventories

The types of materials to be used in an IRI are dictated by the purposes of the inventory itself. Because the establishment of reading levels is one of the expected outcomes of the administration, it is obviously necessary for the materials to represent a variety of levels. In an inventory to be used with children varying in age and ability, for instance, it is usual to have the difficulty level of material progress from preprimer level to the highest point one of the children is likely to need. These materials may represent a variety of subject areas and types of writing. However, if the examiner were interested primarily in the child's achievement levels in the science area, materials relevant to this content field should be used for the inventory. Because an evaluation of competence in handling specific skills and abilities is the desired outcome, the materials of the inventory should present the opportunity for evaluating this competence. Obviously, not every ability which is a part of reading comprehension can be tapped in the course of each inventory; however, an attempt should be made to obtain an adequate sampling.

In choosing the actual passage for inclusion in the inventory, the guiding questions should be: "Does this selection seem similar to most of the selections included in this book?" "Does it allow for sampling the important skills developed at this level of the material?" If the chosen selection is substantially easier or more difficult than most of those included at that level, inappropriate diagnostic conclusions will be drawn. The examiner also must keep in mind that it will be necessary to formulate five to ten comprehension questions based on the content of the selection, or else to have enough content to allow a reflection of the child's understanding of it during retelling. If a selection of very meager content is chosen, it will be extremely difficult—if not impossible—to construct questions or to otherwise evaluate comprehension.

For most individual IRIs, at least two selections from each level are chosen to be tested; one for oral reading and one for silent reading. A third selection at each level is useful for evaluating listening comprehension, and this selection should be parallel with the selections used for oral and silent reading.

There is no clear consensus as to whether the selections used for oral and silent reading should be taken from the same material and thus deal with similar content. When this is done, it seems safer to compare oral and silent reading performance, since the concepts involved in reading are similar. In addition, it seems less likely there would be a meaningful difference in the level of challenge of the two selections. However, some users of IRIs contend that choosing the oral and silent reading passages from two different selections allows for a wider range of skill and concept evaluation. They also argue that reading the oral passage will influence, and perhaps make easier, the comprehension of the silently read passage. While these authors tend to favor using passages from the same selection, the final choice can be made by the teacher constructing the inventory. If connected materials are chosen, one must be careful to see that responses to the comprehension process used for silent reading are truly dependent on that passage and not answerable from the passage used for evaluation of oral reading performance.

The number of levels included in the inventory will depend on the purposes for which the inventory will be used. For example, a first grade teacher might need an inventory ranging only from preprimer through third reader level. The reading specialist working with grades one through six might need selections ranging from preprimer through at least eighth reader level.

In general, the selections used in an IRI should be of increasing length from preprimer through the highest level used. Here again a balance is needed. Short selections present problems for reliably evaluating both word recognition and comprehension skills. Reliability is questionable whenever a small sampling of behavior is made. On the other hand, children tire if lengthy selections are used and several levels of the inventory are administered. While the following guidelines for *approximate* length of IRI selections do not need to be rigidly enforced, they may be used for guidance.

Preprimer to Primer	50-75 words
First Reader to Second Reader	100 words
Third Reader to Fourth Reader	150 words
Fifth Reader to Sixth Reader	200 words
Seventh Reader and Above	250 words

Passages selected for use in evaluating oral and silent reading should be subjected to an indepth analysis to determine if they are rich enough in content to warrant their use. The material also should be carefully analyzed for the overall ideas contained, as well as the specific abilities students will need to successfully handle the material.

The teacher or clinician must read the selection from different viewpoints. To establish an overall set for the approach to evaluation, the material initially should be read from the point of view of the potential examinee rather than from an adult reading specialist. The primary purpose of this first reading would be to get some idea of how children might react to the material and what they might learn from it. The reading should produce a list of anticipated outcomes which will consist of the major concepts included in the passage. (An illustration of the outcome of such an analysis is given later in this chapter.)

Once selections are chosen, a valid procedure is to pilot test them with a group of readers. Having even a few students read and react to selections being considered for use in an IRI can be informative and can save time by revealing unanticipated problems with the material.

A second reading of the selection should be done from the point of view of the professional concerned with evaluating the child's performance. During this reading, notes should be made on the words or phrases which might cause difficulty, abilities which will be called upon in the course of the reading, and any other elements which will need to be a part of the evaluation. From this second reading could come lists of the specific background, skill, concept, vocabulary, and thinking requirements of the selection. If these analyses are done carefully and in detail, the writing of comprehension questions will not be so arduous.

Formulating Questions for Informal Reading Inventories

There is no widespread agreement as to the types of questions that should be included in IRIs; therefore, it is recommended that those constructing IRIs use the simple scheme of classifying questions as factual, inferential, vocabulary, and evaluative. This scheme calls for having factual recall questions—questions which require simple recall of information directly stated by the author in the selection. Inferential questions typically require the reader to manipulate information in a selection to draw a conclusion or to combine information with knowledge already possessed to draw a conclusion. Vocabulary questions simply tap the reader's knowledge of the meaning of words contained in the selection. Evaluative questions require the reader to make a judgment, especially from a particular point of view. Evaluative questions frequently allow for a greater variety of responses than any of the other types listed. Use of evaluative questions requires thoughtful analysis on the part of the teacher. Again, it is important for teachers constructing IRIs to use a scheme for constructing questions that matches their purposes for testing. Research does not support one categorization scheme for questioning over another.

In formulating questions, the teacher should keep in mind a concept labeled *passage dependency.* A passage dependent question is one a reader is not likely to be able to answer based on prior knowledge alone; that is, the question is not apt to be answered correctly unless the content of a selection has been read and understood. For example, "What happens to water when it gets very cold?" is probably not a good question for use with a fourth reader science selection. Most fourth graders could answer such a question without having read the passage; thus, it would be a nonpassage dependent question.

Vocabulary type questions frequently are nonpassage dependent. The suggested guideline here is, a word chosen for a vocabulary question should be one readers seem unlikely to already know and one which is defined, directly or by implication, in the context of the passage read. In addition to avoiding well known words, it also seems inappropriate to ask about a difficult vocabulary item whose meaning is not developed in the passage. If such words occur and their meanings are essential to the comprehension of the passage, it is probably a poor passage for that level.

Another question that provides little information about a reader's comprehension strategies is one which gives students two alternatives. Questions such as, "Did the boy ever get to the library?" or "Was the mother happy or sad at the end of the story?" should not be included. Such questions tend to encourage guessing rather than thoughtful comprehension. Children who understood nothing of what they read would have a 50 percent chance of answering correctly.

The use of evaluative questions requires the reader to make judgments about the content of the materials read. These questions frequently include the phrase, "Do you think?" For example, "Why do you think the boy answered the way he did?" or "What do you think Alice should have done when she found the child?" Definite guidelines are needed for determining an acceptable answer. It would be inappropriate to use evaluative questions that allow credit for any response. To be credited, a response to an evaluative question should 1) be based on information presented in the text and not contradict the information presented; 2) be a logical synthesis of text information and knowledge already possessed by the reader representing some point of view; 3) be capable of verification (a clear basis should exist for judging whether the response is acceptable); and 4) ask readers why they answered as they did.

It is recommended that, wherever possible, the teacher construct ten questions for each selection used. Often this is not possible for the shorter selections at the earliest levels, since these selections repeat the same information. Here again, the concept of reliability appears. Having fewer questions means each question carries more weight. For example, if there are five questions, a child who misses only one falls below the quantitative comprehension criterion for an independent reading level. It is better, however, to use fewer questions than to include inferior questions.

Finally, a balance of factual, inferential, evaluative, and vocabulary questions should be used. It is generally unacceptable to make more than half of the questions any one of the four types.

Illustration of Analysis of Reading Material and Generation of Questions

Now that general guides have been given for the selection and preparation of materials for inventory purposes, the specific ways in which these materials might be treated can be best shown by example. The following selection is one which might have been chosen for inclusion in an inventory. The discussion that follows the selection illustrates how an examiner might analyze the selection and prepare it for inclusion in an IRI. Some discussion of how questions might be prepared is also included.

PENNSYLVANIA

Pennsylvania, with an area of over 45,000 square miles and a population of almost 12 million, is filled with contrast and diversity. It is a state in which almost two-thirds of the population live in urban areas. Philadelphia, with a population approaching two million, is the fifth largest city in the United States. On any weekday, thousands of people in the cities of Pennsylvania hurry to their work in large office buildings, in bustling stores and restaurants, and in noisy factories. Crowded subway cars, trains, and buses move workers from their homes to their jobs. In contrast, Pennsylvania also contains large areas of farmland where life is quieter. Crowds of people and the rush of traffic are absent. In the rural areas of York and Lancaster Counties, rolling hills and fields of tobacco or corn replace sidewalks and office buildings. In some areas of these counties, the farms are worked by Amish farmers, whose lifestyle is in sharp contrast to modern cities. Amish people reject the use of all "modern" developments. In place of cars, they use horses and buggies; in place of tractors, they use mules to pull plows and other farm equipment.

The first and most obvious consideration of this selection is that it is factual and expository. It is often helpful to analyze the way in which information is structured or arranged in material. There is an explicitly stated topic represented in the title, "Pennsylvania," and an explicitly stated main idea, "Pennsylvania is filled with contrast and diversity." A hierarchical arrangement of information follows, indicating that while much of Pennsylvania is urban, it also has a rural side. The paragraph also demonstrates a general structure of contrasting information. First, information is given about urban areas of Pennsylvania; then, the contrast of rural life is presented.

It would be interesting to administer this paragraph using a retelling strategy. Readers who possess good comprehension skills tend to preserve the major structure of a selection when they order the information in their retellings.

The concepts needed to comprehend the selection are primarily geographic or from the social sciences. Specific information, such as the population of Pennsylvania or of Philadelphia, is more likely to be remembered if the reader has some general concepts of the relative population of states and cities. Obviously, concepts of states and counties are needed to make sense of some of the information. Readers unfamiliar with the Amish would have difficulty with the last part of the selection.

Given the general level of difficulty of the paragraph about Pennsylvania, the vocabulary challenge does not appear to be particularly difficult. However, words such as *area, square miles, contrast, diversity, urban, bustling, rural, Amish,* or *buggies* may be unknown by some students.

If a questioning strategy is to be used for administering the IRI containing this selection, questions need to be constructed. The first part of the selection contains many specific facts that might serve as the basis for factual level questions.

Several possibilities exist for more inferential questions. For example, one could call for some mathematical inferencing by asking "Approximately how many Pennsylvanians live in rural areas?" Using the information about Amish farmers given in the passage, would the reader be able to tell about some everyday, taken for granted objects missing from Amish homes? Could readers infer the meaning of the word *urban* from the context of the selection? At the evaluative level, teachers could ask how an Amish person might adjust to life in Philadelphia.

While it has been suggested that vocabulary, factual, inferential, and evaluative classifications be used to generate and order questions, we do not mean to imply that these are always clear cut categories. For example, consider the question, "What is the main idea of this paragraph?" As pointed out earlier, we judge the main idea to be explicitly stated in the paragraph. Does this make it a factual recall item? Couldn't such a question be considered inferential in the sense that readers must combine what they know about main ideas with the information contained in the selection? Likewise, the issue of passage dependency is not always clear. Consider, "What does the word urban mean?" For the child who knew the meaning of urban before reading the selection, it is not passage dependent; for the child who infers its meaning from the passage, it is. The important point is that framing questions for IRIs is not a simple, straightforward activity.

Concluding Statement

By constructing an IRI based on materials available for instructional use, a teacher can avoid many of the pitfalls associated with establishing reading levels and can develop greater sensitivity to evaluating reading. This chapter has provided some general guidelines for selecting materials from which an IRI can be constructed and for formulating questions to be used with selections read orally or silently by a child. In order to construct a useful IRI, thoughtful analysis of the material to be read is necessary.

Chapter 7
Group Informal Reading Inventories

The administration of a group reading inventory requires substantial flexibility and experience. While the guidelines for use of individual IRIs have been presented in great detail, the procedures for group administration of such an inventory are outlined in this chapter in more general terms. Teachers familiar with Directed Reading Activities will find striking similarities between DRAs and group IRIs. The major differences are in purpose. The DRA has as its purpose the teaching of reading; the group IRI has as its purpose the evaluation of reading.

A group IRI should include the same major phases as does the individual inventory—readiness, evaluation of word recognition ability, reading per se, and listening. Some of this work may be done on an individual basis, even though the inventory is basically administered with a group.

Teacher Readiness

The first step for evaluating in group situations is to make an estimate of the possible instructional level of each child. Many kinds of data can be obtained from cumulative records, previous teachers, standardized test scores, and observations of daily performance. These sources supply the information on which the hypothesis is made about the probable instructional level of each student. In a sixth grade class, a teacher may tentatively decide that one group is ready for instruction at fourth reader level, another at fifth, a third at sixth, and a fourth somewhere above sixth. In addition, the teacher may feel that four of the pupils are far below the others in achievement, but may be uncertain about definite levels.

The teacher might select reading material at sixth reader level and prepare it for use as an inventory. The selection should be one that could be used for an instructional reading activity. Preparation would include analyzing the material for vocabulary, word recognition demands, and required thinking abilities. When preparation is complete, the teacher is ready to begin the inventory for those whose instructional levels are estimated to be approximately sixth reader level. A similar selection of appropriate materials would have to be made at other estimated levels, and the teacher would have to make thorough preparations for each. Under this plan, the inventory would proceed as a series of evaluative

DRAs in which the emphasis would be on observation of children's ability to handle the materials, rather than on teaching procedures.

Conducting the Group Reading Inventory

When the group is assembled for the inventory, the overall plan will vary little from that for any good instructional DRA. The differences lie in matters of emphasis. The objective is not to teach, but to determine if the material would be suitable for teaching. The basic question to be answered is "Can children profit from instruction in this material?" Each phase of the reading activity must be directed toward evaluation. Actual teaching is done only to see how well various individuals respond to instruction at this level. Thus, any instruction given in the inventory situation is actually for purposes of further evaluation.

Pupil preparation. The teacher may use a variety of techniques and materials during the readiness or preparatory part of the group inventory. The objectives are 1) to evaluate the pupils' background of relevant experiences and their ability to use those experiences, 2) to see how many relevant concepts pupils have at their disposal, 3) to determine whether pupils have a grasp of the vocabulary used in this material to express essential concepts, 4) to evaluate pupils' ability to perform the thinking processes involved in understanding the selection, and 5) to determine the degree of interest pupils show. These same objectives guide the evaluative phase of an instructional activity. In both inventory and instructional activity, the objectives will be achieved only if the teacher allows freedom for the pupils to reveal their interests, concepts, vocabularies, experiences, and thinking abilities. The teacher's knowledge of the children's backgrounds, materials read previously, pictures accompanying the material to be read currently, and concrete objects rich in stimulus value should stimulate group discussions. If it seems desirable to find out what and how pupils think, the teacher must ask more than tell, tentatively accept ideas even though they may be wrong, record contributions for further work, use vocabulary from the material to see how pupils respond, or set up situations which demand the same thinking abilities and processes required to understand the material.

No attempt would be made to fill all the gaps discovered in the inventory. For some of the pupils taking the inventory, deficiencies in experience, vocabulary, concepts, or thinking abilities might be so severe that instruction in this material would be impossible. For these children, the essential question has already been answered; sixth reader level is too difficult for instructional use. Depending on the classroom situation at the moment, these students might be dropped from the reading inventory to go on with some other activity or might continue the inventory even though no more evaluation is necessary at this level. If pupils continue, the teacher is obligated to see that it is not a frustrating experience and that their inability to function is not evident to others in the group.

For those pupils who seem able to proceed with the material, the preparatory phase would continue with some developmental work. Clarification or development of concepts, introduction of essential vocabulary, and guidance in thinking processes might be undertaken. Students would be guided toward the establishment of purposes for reading. This would be done to further the evaluation, to see how well children can profit from this help and apply it during the rest of the activity. During this stage of the inventory, the teacher might assume a directive role in order to identify specific points which need to be developed.

Silent reading. Once preparation has been completed and purposes for reading established, the second phase of the activity begins. Pupils read the material silently to satisfy the purposes. Now the teacher has an opportunity to observe their performance. Some may proceed with no difficulty – reading at an acceptable rate, reflecting their understanding in their expression, stopping when they have achieved what they set out to do. Others may exhibit various symptoms of difficulty – frowning, lip moving, finger pointing, or requesting frequent help. Some may take an inordinate amount of time as they struggle along. All the things the teacher sees and hears during this silent reading period will become part of the data on which to base the final evaluation. From the questions asked and the comments made, much may be learned about strengths and weaknesses in pupil performance.

Discussion and rereading. When the silent reading has been completed, group discussion will focus on the purposes established for reading, and the teacher will have an opportunity to discover how well various individuals satisfied those purposes. Both oral and silent rereading may occur spontaneously or on teacher request. Appraisal can be made of oral reading performance and the ability to determine the relevancy of ideas. Questions other than those raised in the original purposes can be asked to allow for more complete evaluation of each students' understanding of the material and the way in which word recognition problems are handled.

Conclusions and follow up. By the time the preparatory phase, silent reading, discussion, and rereading have been completed, the teacher should have some evidence of each child's ability or inability to profit from instruction at this level. Additional information will have been gained about those who can function adequately at that level with instructional aid. The teacher may have noted that one student had difficulty getting meaning from a context clue expressed in an appropriate phrase; another had trouble with two vowels together when they were in two separate syllables; and a third encountered trouble with a sentence based on order of importance. In other words, the teacher may have discovered some of the specific needs of the pupils who are going to receive instruction at sixth reader level. At the same time, much was probably learned about the strengths of these students, what they were able to do well, and the readiness they had for additional learning.

The teacher may know that pupils who handled everything independently, spontaneously, and virtually perfectly at sixth reader level need to be checked at a higher level. Instructional needs were not seen because they are not evident at this independent level. Pupils for whom this material was too difficult need to be reevaluated at a lower level. Their skills and abilities could not be appraised because the children were in so much trouble they were unable to apply the skills they did have.

During succeeding periods, the same procedures would be followed with other materials. Pupils for whom sixth reader materials had been too difficult might join groups being checked at fourth or fifth; those for whom sixth had been too easy might be checked at seventh or eighth. After all group inventories have been completed, additional information might be needed on some pupils and, at that time, individual inventories would be administered. This might mean making special arrangements outside the classroom setting.

Informal Word Recognition Tests As Supplements to Group Informal Reading Inventories

In the classroom situation, it may not be necessary to administer a word recognition test to each child. It is highly possible the teacher might obtain sufficient information on most children's level of functioning in this area through the reading inventory and normal classroom activities. In some cases, a more thorough analysis of specific word identification strengths and weaknesses might be needed; in others, an estimate of ability to handle the word recognition burden of particular instructional materials might be helpful. In either case, an inventory of the child's range of immediate recognition vocabulary and ability to apply word analysis skills is in order. A sampling of the vocabulary of specific materials being considered for instructional use would be appropriate.

Even when it is part of an overall group reading inventory, the word recognition inventory should be administered to one child at a time. There is no group technique for obtaining the necessary information about the child's level of achievement on such a test. The specific procedures could be the same as those of the word recognition inventory discussed under the procedures for individual administration included in Chapter 4.

Group Listening Comprehension Inventory

A child's hearing comprehension can be determined through group procedures similar to those used for the reading inventory. Actually, the group listening inventory is an evaluatively oriented directed listening activity.

Teacher preparation. In this area, information is available which can serve as a base for the setting of a tentative level. Children's reactions to class discussion, conversation, or materials read to the group in the course of normal class activity will provide clues to their probable level of functioning in listening situations.

Materials at levels comparable to these estimated levels should be selected for the listening inventory. Analyses of these materials, in preparation for working with them in the group situation, must proceed in the same fashion as preparation for the reading inventory. Word recognition is no longer of concern. There must be acquaintance with the material from the standpoint of its conceptual burden and the thinking abilities it acquires.

Presentation to pupils. Readiness for effective listening is as necessary as readiness for reading. Consequently, adequate evaluation of children's readiness to listen profitably to the chosen material must be the first step of the inventory. Purposes for listening must be established. When pupil preparation has been completed, guided listening proceeds with the teacher reading the material. This would be followed by an evaluatively oriented discussion of the selection planned to reveal the children's level of understanding of the author's ideas.

Conclusion and follow up. On the basis of observations made during the readiness period, the actual listening, and the ensuing discussion, tentative decisions can be made about each child's hearing comprehension level. For some in the group, rather definite conclusions may have been drawn about the specific level at which they can be instructed in listening activities. For others, further inventories may be indicated, with the whole process having to be repeated with appropriate materials at varying levels of difficulty.

Concluding Statement

The concept of IRIs can be applied to evaluating the reading and listening skills of groups of students. The procedures and steps used in group informal reading inventories are similar to those used in the instructional plan for a directed reading activity. The major difference between DRAs and group IRIs lies in the major purpose of the two: instruction compared to evaluation. There are numerous similarities between group and individual IRIs. Economy of time is the major advantage of group IRIs. Group evaluation may be the only approach feasible when sizable numbers of students need to be tested. The major limitation of group IRIs is that the teacher loses the opportunity to make closer observations. However, group inventories can serve to provide useful tentative information which can be supplemented with data from individual word recognition tests or individual informal reading inventories administered to students for whom additional evaluation is needed.

Chapter 8
Conclusions

There is a tendency in the field of reading education to seek simple answers to complex questions. Nowhere does this seem more obvious than in the evaluation of reading performance or skills.

The search goes on, among over 250 reading tests in print, to find *the* test which will offer *the* answer. Our experience is that all commercially prepared tests have enormous limitations in providing answers to the day-to-day questions teachers of reading must answer in order to make appropriate instructional decisions. The goal of this publication is to provide teachers and reading specialists with a set of guidelines for carefully, diagnostically analyzing students' reading behavior – informal reading inventories.

IRIs are not a set of materials; they are an approach to evaluation which can be flexibly applied to provide useful answers to questions about instructional placement, growth in reading achievement, and areas of strengths and weaknesses in reading. The best informal reading inventories possess the following important characteristics.

- *IRIs attempt to evaluate reading through procedures that are as close as possible to useful, natural reading activities.* Rather than using multiple choice or completion items, IRIs require students to read connected text; they attempt to assess comprehension in a fashion similar to the way in which it is typically assessed in classrooms – through questioning strategies or retellings.

- *IRIs attempt to achieve a close fit between assessment and instructional materials.* In their best form, IRIs are constructed by sampling potential instructional materials. Assessment materials are, in effect, portions of that instructional material.

- *IRIs are flexibly used by teachers and reading specialists to answer specific instructional questions or to efficiently understand the nature of a child's reading.* The content of the preceding chapters and of the Appendix attempts to stress that there are a sizable number of facets to an IRI and not all facets need to be used (or used in a specific sequence) with each child. For example, if testing has already yielded enough information about a particular child's level and nature of oral reading ability, the use of oral reading in an inventory can be dropped and attention focused on silent reading at subsequent levels.

- *Effective use of IRIs depends upon examiners who have a good understanding of the nature of the reading process and are familiar with their flexible, diagnostic use.* While the mechanics of administering and scoring IRIs are relatively simple, their skillful, efficient use and their valid interpretation depend on competent examiners – who have well formulated concepts of the reading process and have learned to use an IRI to gain insight into how students are meeting the challenge of learning to use that process.
- *The results of an IRI are viewed as tentative.* Conclusions reached through the administration of an IRI must be confirmed or modified as a child moves from a testing to an instructional setting. We are confident that IRIs are useful and are among the most reliable and valid approaches to evaluating reading; however, we readily acknowledge IRIs are imperfect.

No ready made inventories, individual or group, have been included in this publication. Some of the items listed in the bibliography do contain or refer to such inventories. However, while such inventories are often useful, limited benefits accrue from using any already prepared inventory. The likelihood is small of finding an already prepared inventory to meet a particular teacher's needs at a specified moment. Far greater impact on both diagnostic and instructional work is apt to be felt when *construction* of inventories, and not merely *administration* of inventories, is experienced. Teachers will learn a lot through successive experiences with their own inventory materials. Careful selection and preparation of materials, followed by tryouts of the inventory with children and resultant modifications, serve as excellent learning experiences. They lead the teacher or reading specialist to feel more in command of the test and the testing. Those who have constructed IRIs appear to better understand their use, their strengths, and their limitations. When a teacher is not dependent on a ready made inventory (or any other test for that matter), there is freedom to go in any needed direction. When determining a child's instructional level in social studies materials, a social studies oriented inventory can be constructed and used. When science is the content area of concern, an inventory based on science text materials is possible. There is no need to infer achievement in one area from what has been achieved in another.

Finally, through skillful, flexible use of IRIs the spirit and practice of diagnostic teaching should begin to pervade classroom reading activities. A teacher who has constructed and mastered the use of reading inventories can hardly ignore the minute by minute, day by day opportunities for informal evaluations of pupils' performances. Each instructional period becomes part of a continuing diagnosis of existing strengths and weaknesses. When this occurs, appropriate instruction can be planned and provided with decreasing need for formal testing procedures. The concept of diagnostic teaching becomes fully employed and the misuses and artificiality that so commonly pervade testing diminish and may be eliminated.

Bibliography

Allington, Richard L. Teacher ability in recording oral reading performance. *Academic Therapy,* 1978, *14,* 187-192.

Barr, Rebecca. Beginning reading instruction from a developmental perspective. In P. David Pearson (Ed.), *Handbook of reading research.* New York: Longman, 1984.

Beldin, H.O. Informal reading testing: Historical review and review of the research. In William K. Durr (Ed.), *Reading difficulties: Diagnosis, correction, and remediation.* Newark, DE: International Reading Association, 1970.

Berliner, David. Academic learning time and reading achievement. In J. Guthrie (Ed.), *Comprehension and teaching: Research reviews.* Newark, DE: International Reading Association, 1981.

Betts, Emmett. *Foundations of reading instruction.* New York: American Book, 1946.

Bristow, Page, Pikulski, John, and Pelosi, Peter. A comparison of five estimates of instructional level. *The Reading Teacher,* 1983, *37,* 273-279.

Buros Institute of Mental Measurements. *Tests in print III.* Lincoln, NE: University of Nebraska Press, 1983.

Carroll, John, Davies, Peter, and Richman, Barry. *The American heritage word frequency book.* Boston: Houghton Mifflin, 1971.

Goodman, Kenneth. Miscues: Windows on the reading process. In Kenneth Goodman (Ed.), *Miscue analysis: Applications to reading instruction.* Urbana, IL: Eric Clearinghouse on Reading and Communication, 1973.

Goodman, Yetta, and Burke, Carolyn. *Reading miscue inventory manual.* New York: Macmillan, 1972.

Horowitz, Rosalind, and Samuels, S. Jay. Reading and listening to expository text. *Journal of Reading Behavior,* 1985, *17,* 18-198.

Johnson, Marjorie S., and Kress, Roy A. *Informal reading inventories.* Newark, DE: International Reading Association, 1965.

Jongsma, Kathleen, and Jongsma, Eugene. Test review: Commercial informal reading inventories. *Reading Teacher,* 1981, *34,* 697-705.

Kibby, Michael W. Passage readability affects the oral reading strategies of disabled readers. *Reading Teacher,* 1979, *32,* 390-396.

Killgallon, P.A. *A study of relationships among certain pupil adjustments in reading situations.* Doctoral dissertation, Pennsylvania State University, 1942.

Lamberg, Walter J., Rodriquez, Laura, and Thomas, Douglas. *Training in identifying oral reading departure from text which can be explained as Spanish-English phonological differences.* Paper presented at the annual meeting of the Southwest Educational Research Association, Austin, Texas, 1978.

Lesgold, A., and Resnick, Lauren. How reading difficulties develop: Perspectives from a longitudinal study. In J.P. Das, R.F. Mulcahy, and A.E. Walls (Eds.), *Theory and research in learning disabilities.* New York: Plenum, 1982.

Leslie, Lauren, and Osol, Pat. Changes in oral reading strategies as a function of qualities of miscue. *Journal of Reading Behavior,* 1978, *10,* 442-444.

Leu, Donald. Oral reading error analysis: A critical review of research and application. *Reading Research Quarterly,* 1982, *17,* 420-437.

Marshall, N., and Glock, M.D. Comprehension of connected discourse: A study into the relationship between the structure of text and information recalled. *Reading Research Quarterly,* 1978-1979, *14,* 10-56.

McKenna, Michael. Informal reading inventories: A review of the issues. *The Reading Teacher,* 1983, *35,* 670-679.

Meyer, Bonnie, and Rice, Elizabeth. The structure of text. In P. David Pearson (Ed.), *Handbook of reading research*. New York: Longman, 1984, 319-352.

Misuse of grade equivalents: Resolution passed by the Delegates Assembly of the International Reading Association, April 1981. *The Reading Teacher*, 1982, *4*, 64.

Page, William D., and Carlson, Kenneth L. The process of observing oral reading scores. *Reading Horizons*, 1975, *15*, 147-150.

Pikulski, John J. Informal reading inventories: A critical review. *The Reading Teacher*, 1974, *28*, 141-151.

Pikulski, John J., and Shanahan, Timothy. Informal reading inventories: A critical analysis. In J. Pikulski and T. Shanahan (Eds.), *Approaches to the informal evaluation of reading*. Newark, DE: International Reading Association, 1982.

Pikulski, John J., and Tobin, Aileen W. The cloze procedure as an informal assessment technique. In J. Pikulski and T. Shanahan (Eds.), *Approaches to the informal evaluation of reading*. Newark, DE: International Reading Association, 1982.

Roe, Michael, and Aiken, Robert. A CAI simulation program for teaching IRI techniques. *Journal of Computer Based Instruction*, 1976, *2*, 52-56.

Schell, Leo (Ed.). *Diagnostic and criterion referenced reading tests: Review and evaluation*. Newark, DE: International Reading Association, 1981.

Spache, George. *Diagnosing and correcting reading disabilities*. Boston: Allyn and Bacon, 1976.

Sticht, Thomas, and James, James. Listening and reading. In P. David Pearson (Ed.), *Handbook of reading research*. New York: Longman, 1984, 293-318.

Williamson, Leon E., and Young, Freda. The IRI and RMI diagnostic concepts should be synthesized. *Journal of Reading Behavior*, 1974, *6*, 183-194.

Appendix
Case Examples: Allison, Jeff, and Carol

The materials in this appendix are designed to be fairly comprehensive reports and interpretations of the results of the administration of IRIs to three children. Chapter 2 discussed some of the major considerations needed when using an IRI to estimate a child's independent, instructional, and frustration levels. The discussion of these three cases illustrates how numerical criteria and qualitative considerations are combined to estimate reading and listening levels. Chapter 4 discussed how oral and silent reading, comprehension performance, and oral reading activities could be used to go beyond establishing levels in order to derive diagnostic information. The materials in this Appendix are intended to illustrate some of those diagnostic possibilities.

Preparing materials for this Appendix proved to be a formidable challenge since we are accustomed to using IRIs in a flexible, ongoing way rather than reaching what may seem like final conclusions. In an ongoing diagnostic/teaching setting, it is best to draw initial impressions from IRIs and then to compare these conclusions with other test data and ongoing observations of the child being evaluated. The space available in this volume clearly prohibits such a comprehensive treatment of the results of an IRI. Nevertheless, sizable portions of the IRI test materials administered to three children—Allison, Jeff, and Carol—have been reproduced so you can compare the record of each child's performance with the conclusions we have drawn. In carefully studying these test materials, you might decide we have emphasized the wrong points, or have omitted significant observations. To a great extent, the interpretations one draws from an IRI reflect biases about what the process of reading is and what factors influence behavior. Thoughtful differences in the interpretation of IRIs are to be expected and, in fact, encouraged.

The content of this chapter has been sequenced to encourage you to draw your own conclusions about the reading performances of three children before we present our conclusions. After you read the background information and review some of the testing results, we encourage you to think about how you might use this information to answer some of the educational questions facing the teacher who administered the IRI. Think about the child's scores as related to the criteria for independent, instructional, frustration, and listening comprehension levels, but do not reach any firm conclusions about those levels based only on numerical criteria. Use the test score summaries to establish a framework for looking diagnostically at the reading performance recorded more fully in the actual test materials. In some cases, the summary of test scores has been deliberately delayed until after some record of the child's performance has been presented in order to more fully encourage the use of qualitative information.

Most of the oral and silent reading selections for the levels of the IRI administered and the questions designed to evaluate the child's comprehension of those selections have been reproduced. Passages have been marked to record oral reading performance and answers to questions. Other examiner comments of behavior observed during the test also may be included.

As you read through the three cases, you will notice the format for presenting the information is different for each one. This was done deliberately to show that the way one looks at IRI results will vary from individual to individual.

The reading passages, and comprehension questions accompanying the passages, used in this Appendix to illustrate how IRIs are interpreted were not chosen because they represent an ideal IRI; they were chosen because they were available and there were no copyright obstacles to their use in this volume. These materials reflect many of the limitations frequently found in teacher constructed IRIs. It is appropriate that you recognize such limitations and respond critically.

For the first two cases reviewed, Allison and Jeff, a discussion of the results follows the presentation of the record of the entire IRI administered. The third case, Carol, is treated in greater detail with a discussion of her performance coming after each level.

To facilitate the interpretation of the materials that follow, the reader might wish to review the symbols previously recommended for recording responses to IRIs and individual word recognition tests.

Case Study #1: Allison

Background Information

Allison transferred to a new school at the beginning of the academic year of sixth grade. Records received by her new teacher indicated that Allison had been in the average reading group in fifth grade and had completed a fifth reader level book. However, the reading program used to instruct Allison was different from the one being used in her new school. Allison was one of only three new students in her class; therefore, Allison's new teacher decided to administer an IRI to obtain additional information about the appropriate reading instruction group for Allison and to determine if any specific areas of instructional need might emerge.

Testing Information

Because records indicated Allison had completed a fifth level reading text successfully, the teacher administered the IRI at fifth reader level. The teacher then tested oral and silent reading at both sixth and seventh reader levels. Finally, listening comprehension was evaluated at seventh and eighth grade levels.

Summary of Allison's IRI Scores

Reading

Level	Oral Reading in Context	% Oral Comprehension	% Silent Comprehension	% Average Comprehension
Fifth	98	80	100	90
Sixth	97	73	91	82
Seventh	94	30		

Listening

Level	% Comprehension
Seventh	80
Eighth	50

Protocol Materials for Allison

Fifth Reader Level: Oral Selection

(84")

218 words

Alexander Graham Bell was born in Scotland. His mother was a painter, and his father taught deaf people ~~how~~ to speak. Bell became very interested in his father's work. He and his two brothers began to hcip their father with his work. In order to learn more about how to help deaf people speak, Bell began to study how speech sounds *were* ~~are~~ made.

When Bell was twenty-three years old his family moved to Canada. A year later Bell moved again and opened a school for teachers *for* ~~of~~ deaf children in the United States. At his school he studied more about how sounds were made. Then he started to look for a way to send the *sounds* ~~sound~~ of people's voices long distances. Other people had found ways to send noise, music, and signals long distances over wires, but no one had been able to find a way to send people's voices over wires. People began sending messages to each other by using the telegraph, but they still could not talk to each other. Bell decided he would try to find a way to let people who were not in the same place talk to each other.

$$218 \overline{\smash{\big)}\ 4.000} \quad .01802\%$$

$$\begin{array}{r} 100_2 \\ -2 \\ \hline 98\% \end{array}$$

Questions for Fifth Reader Level: Oral Selection and Allison's Responses

✓1. Where was Alexander Graham Bell born? (Scotland)

✓2. From what you read, how many people do you think were in the Bell family? (5 - or at least 5) *Two brothers, parents + him — That's 5 I guess*

✓3. How do you think Alexander Bell became interested in helping deaf people to speak? (His father introduced him to the work.)
   Probably from his father. That's what he did.

✗4. How old was Bell when he opened a school for teachers of the deaf? (24)
   I don't remember.

✓5. Name three countries where Bell had lived. (Scotland, Canada, the United States)

✓6. What did the article say Bell started to study in order to learn more about how to help deaf people talk? (how speech sounds were made)
   The way speech was made Q you know, sounds.

✓7. What did Bell try after he learned about how speech sounds are made? (to send the sound of voices long distances)
   To invent the telephone

✓8. What was invented first, the telephone or the telegraph? How do you know? (telegraph - said people could send messages with it but couldn't send the sound of voices) *Telegraph — said it sent messages but Bell hadn't invented telephone yet*

✓9. Name two types of sounds that could be sent over wires before peoples' voices could. (any two: noise, music, and signals)

✗10. Once Bell became interested in finding a way to send voices long distances, did he spend all of his time trying to find a way? How do you know? (no, said he spent his time teaching also) *Don't think so. Can't remember what it said.* 80%

89

At his school for teachers of the deaf, Alexander Graham Bell began working with a friend named Tom Watson. Tom also wanted to find a way to send the sound of the human voice long distances. Bell and Watson worked for many years. Bell was a teacher during the day, and Tom worked all day in a shop. The only time they could work on their project was at night. After much work they did find a way to send the human voice over wires. When Bell was twenty-nine years old, he and Watson invented the telephone. Bell was the first one to talk on it. His first words were to Tom. *ORR* He said, "Mr. Watson, come here, I want you."

Bell called Tom because he needed Tom's help. Bell had spilled acid on himself, and it was burning his clothes. He was really very surprised when Tom came running in. He wasn't badly burned, but neither of them ever forgot the words Bell spoke.

After they found the way to send the human voice long distances, Bell went back to trying to help deaf people learn to speak. Bell's wife was deaf, and this may have made him even more interested in helping the deaf to speak.

58"

Questions for Fifth Reader Level: Silent Selection and Allison's Responses

✓1. What were the names of the two people who were talked about most in this story? (Bell and Watson)

✓2. Why might you think that neither Watson nor Bell was very rich? (both had to work) *Bell was a teacher + they had to work at night.*

✓3. What did the men in this story invent? (the telephone)

✓4. How old was Bell when he invented the telephone? (29)

✓5. Who was the first person to talk on the telephone? (Bell)

✓6. What were the first words spoken on a telephone? (Mr. Watson, come here, I want you—acceptable paraphrase)

✓7. Why might you think Bell was very excited when he said "Mr. Watson, come here, I want you"? (He had spilled acid, and it was burning his clothes.)

✓8. Did Bell expect the telephone to work when it did? How do you know? (no, it said he was surprised) *He seemed surprised when Watson came.*

✓9. What did Bell do after he invented the telephone? (returned to helping deaf people learn to speak) *Started working as teacher again Q Deaf people to talk*

✓10. What might have made Bell especially interested in helping deaf people? (His wife was deaf.) *Wanted to especially help his wife*

100%

Oral Rereading

Read the part of the selection that gives the first words spoken on the telephone.

Camels are sometimes called the ~~ships~~ *stripes* of the desert. This is a good name for

this rather ~~odd~~ *old* looking/creature. Without camels people could not have traveled

across the great ~~deserts~~ *desert* of Asia and Africa nearly as early as ~~they~~ *we* did.

The camel is far from being a handsome animal. It has a head that ~~seems~~ *is* too

small for its body and eyes which have very heavy lids and which seem to stick

out from its head. Its neck is so long that it curves. Camels ~~have~~ *are* thick, rough

lips, and have very rough looking, shaggy fur.

Everything about the way the camel looks seems to be important for letting the

camel live in the desert. The heavy eyelids protect the camel from the very bright

sunlight of the desert. The eyes, which seem to stick out, let the camel see for

very long distances. With its long neck the camel can reach food in trees as well

as on the ground. With its thick, rough lips it can eat the hard, sometimes sharp

plants that grow in the desert. The shaggy, heavy coat of the camel protects it

from the heat of the desert during the day and the cold at night.

(56")

$$203\overline{)6.000} \quad .029 \text{ or } 3\%$$

$$100 - 3 = 97\%$$

Questions for Sixth Reader Level: Oral Selections and Allison's Responses

✓1. What did most of the article tell about? (how body of the camel is well suited to desert life) *About how camels look Q about how their body lets them live in the desert*

✓2. Why are camels called ships of the desert? (They are the means that allowed people to cross deserts.) *People used them to travel over deserts.*

✗3. On what two continents were camels used to cross deserts? (Asia and Africa) *DK*

✗4. What is unusual about a camel's face? (too small for its body) *Ugly Q not nice*

✓5. What does the word protrude mean? (stick out) *point out*

✓6. How are the camel's eyes protected from the sunlight? (thick eyelids)

✓7. What one thing about a camel might allow it to live in a cold place? (thick coat) *shaggy coat*

✓8. Why might you think camels eat lots of different things? (selection said a camel can eat from trees and the ground) *Eats lots of plants from trees and on ground*

✓9. Do you think camels eat plants or meat or both plants and meat? What in this article makes you think so? (Everything mentioned was a plant.) *Talked about eating plants*

✗10. Why might you think camels have very strong teeth? (mentioned that they ate hard and sharp plants) *Don't remember anything about its teeth*

✓11. Why might you think that temperatures on the desert change quite a bit in a 24 hour day? (hot during the day, cold at night) *It's gets cold at night — very hot in day.*

$$\frac{100}{-27}$$ 73 %

Sixth Reader Level: Silent Selection   233 words

Camels can go for long periods of time without food or water. There are some stories that say camels have traveled without water for over thirty days. Usually camels can go without water for only five or six days, but they can go longer if there are juicy plants for them to eat. Many people think camels store water in the one or two humps they have on their backs, but this is not true. Camels have no special place to store water. The reason camels need so little water is that they do not use much water to cool their bodies. Most animals cool their bodies by sweating, which uses up water, but camels do not. Camels are also important animals in the desert because they can "smell" water from far away. Some people say they can smell water from as far away as thirty miles.

— ORR

The humps on the camel's back are made of fat. They are not part of the camel's backbone. The fat in the camel's hump is food the camel stores for when it is hungry and there is no food around. If a camel goes for many days without food, the humps become very small or almost disappear. *Good location + oral rereading skills — comparable to 5th reader performance*

There are only two kinds of camels in the world. Arabian camels are camels with one hump on their backs. Bactrian camels, which live in Asia, have two humps.

63″

Questions for Sixth Reader: Silent Selection and Allison's Responses

✓1. What did most of this selection tell about camels? (how they can go without water and food for long distances) *How they look — about their humps and about going without water for days and days*

✓2. How long do some stories say camels can go without water? (30 days)

✓3. Why does the kind of food the camel eats make a difference as to how long it can go without water? (if food contains water they can go longer without water) *Plants with lots of water are good.*

✓4. Why might a thirsty traveler be willing to follow a thirsty camel? (Camels are said to be able to "smell" water from far away.) *Said camels smell water but water doesn't really smell*

✓5. Why do camels need so little water? (they lose very little through sweat) *They don't sweat.*

✓6. Why might you think that camels might get very hot? (said animals cool themselves by sweating and that camels don't sweat) *They don't sweat — sweating makes you cool yourself.*

✓7. What does the word <u>store</u> mean in the selection you read? (to put away for future use) *Keep for later.*

✓8. What is the hump of a camel made of? (fat or food) *Food stored for when it's hungry*

✓9. What can you tell about a camel with a very large hump? (has had plenty to eat) *It's full — not gone days without eating*

✓10. What is different between the two kinds of camels? (number of humps) *One or two humps*

✗11. Where do Bactrian camels live? (Asia) *africa*   91%

Oral Rereading

Read the sentences that tell you something about the humps on a camel's back.

95

China has over three times as many people living in it than does the United States, but China is only slightly larger in size. Parts of China are very overcrowded because most of the people live in ~~it~~ about one third of ~~that~~ *the* country's space. Most of the people of China are farmers, but much of the land is not ~~suitable~~ *used* for farming. The richest farm land is around the Yangtze river. There are other areas of China with good soil, but in many cases they are not as productive because of insufficient rainfall or harsh long winters.

The climate in China is extreme*ly* in most places, either too hot or too cold depending on the season. This results from the fact that China is mostly surrounded by land, with no large bodies of water in it. Water heats and cools much more slowly than does land. The eastern part of China borders the Yellow Sea and the South China Sea. Here the temperatures are more ~~moderate, neither as~~ *modern and newer and* hot in the summer ~~nor~~ *and* as cold in *the* winter.

China contains large land areas where people cannot live. Much of the Northern border of China is desert, and the great Takla Maken Desert *Těkalama* in the west is so dry and so large that few people, even in modern times, have ever crossed it.

$$\left(82''\right)$$

$$194\overline{)12.000} \quad \frac{.061\ or\ 6\%}{}$$
$$\underline{11\ 64}$$
$$3\ 6\ 0$$
$$1\ 9\ 4$$

$$\frac{100}{6}$$
$$\overline{94\%}$$

Questions for Seventh Reader Level: Oral Selection and Allison's Responses

X 1. How does the size of China compare with the size of the United States? (China is slightly larger) *They're the same*

X 2. What do most Chinese people do for a living? (farm) *Factories*

X 3. Why are parts of China especially overcrowded? (Most of the people live in a third of the country.) *Too many people Q DK*

X 4. Why might you expect to find many people living around the Yangtze River? (richest farm land there) *Cooler there*

√ 5. Why are some parts of China which have rich soil not good for farming? (long winters, insufficient rainfall) *Cold and Dry*

X 6. Why might you think that travel by boat would not be an important form of transportation for traveling in China? (no large bodies of water) *DK*

√ 7. How do large bodies of water affect the climate of a country? (make temperatures more moderate) *Water cools and heats slower — not as hot or cold*

√ 8. What does <u>moderate</u> mean? (not extreme; in this article, neither too hot nor too cold) *Not too hot or cold — in between*

X 9. What two seas border the eastern part of China? (Yellow Sea and South China Sea) *Don't remember*

X 10. What kind of land is found in the north and west of China? (desert) *Farm land* 30%

Note to reader: Because Allison's oral reading in context performance seemed weak and because of her very poor performance in comprehension on the orally read selection at this level, the silent selection was not administered. Instead, a seventh reader selection was administered to assess listening comprehension.

Listening Comprehension Selections

Selections of seventh and eighth grade reader level difficulties were read by the examiner to Allison, and she was asked ten comprehension questions per selection.

Seventh Reader Level: Listening Selection

The geography of North China is so different from South China that people sometimes refer to the existence of two Chinas. North China is sometimes called the brown North because water is scarce, the land is dusty, and green plants can grow for only a few months out of the year. There is abundant rainfall in South China which is sometimes called the green South. The soil is rich and multiple crops can be produced in a year. In the North millet, wheat, and beans are the principal crops. In the South wheat is grown and rice is popular, but a wide variety of crops are grown.

City life in the North and South is also quite different. Cities in the North are spread out and the wide streets often seem nearly empty. In the South, the narrow streets are filled with people buying things from shops. Markets display all kinds of vegetables, fruits, and fish. In the cities of both the North and South there are many tea shops, which are a favorite meeting place for Chinese people.

The people of the North and South are also different from one another. The people in the South tend to be very quick in the way they act and the way they speak. The people in the North are more relaxed and move and speak much more slowly.

Questions for Seventh Reader Level: Listening Selection and Allison's Responses

✓1. What was this article mostly about? What was the topic? (differences between North and South China) *How North and South China differ*

✓2. Why do people sometimes say there are two Chinas? (The North and South are so different they hardly seem the same country.) *They're so different, they seem like two countries*

✓3. Why is North China called the brown North? (land is dusty, probably looks brown because of lack of green plants) *Dusty — things don't grow well*

✓4. What does <u>abundant</u> mean? (plentiful) *Lots of it*

✗5. Why might you think that millet does not require a great deal of water to grow? (It's one of the principal crops of the North where water is scarce.) *OK Not sure what millet is*

✓6. In what part of China would you expect to find larger cities? Why? (south, more food is available to support a larger population) *In south — more food*

✓7. What two things would make driving a car in a city in South China particularly difficult? (streets are narrow and very crowded)

✗8. Where do Chinese people like to meet? (in tea shops) *In crowded streets*

✓9. Describe how the people in the South compare to the people in the North. (people from South act and talk more quickly, people from North are more relaxed) *South people talk faster — more energy*

✓10. Why do you think people in the North of China act so different from people in the South? (any reasonable answer reflecting the different way of life in the two parts of the country) *They just keep going — work life is different there* **80%**

Oral Rereading

Read the sentence which tells about something that is the same in both North and South China.

Eighth Reader Level: Listening Selection

The Civil War, which began in 1861 and lasted four years, is also known as the War between the States. It was a war between the Northern and Southern states of the United States over the issue of slavery. Southern states needed slaves to work on large farms, but slaves were not needed in the factories and cities of the North. Many Northerners came to feel that slavery was wrong and that no one had a right to own another human being. In November 1860, Abraham Lincoln was elected president of the United States. Many people in the South thought he would try to make slavery illegal in all the states. In fact, when the lawmakers of South Carolina learned that he was elected president, they began taking steps to have the state become separate from the United States government. In December 1860, at a state convention, the people of South Carolina decided to secede from, leave, the government of the United States. In February 1861, six other states joined in setting up a new nation—the Confederate States of America. Lincoln warned these states that they could not leave the United States and what they were doing would lead to war. In April 1862, the Confederate States tried to take over Fort Sumter from the United States, and the war began.

Questions for Eighth Reader Level: Listening Selection and Allison's Responses

X 1. What year did the Civil War end? (1865)

Don't remember

X 2. By what other name was the Civil War known? (War between the States)

The slave war

✓ 3. What was a major cause of the Civil War? (disagreement over slavery)

Slaves— some didn't want them, some did

X 4. During this period, in what part of the United States do you think most food was grown? (South, most farms there)

Didn't say Q DK

X 5. Why weren't slaves important in the North? (weren't used in the factories)

People liked them Q DK

✓ 6. Do you think many Southerners voted for Abraham Lincoln to become president? Why? (no, they favored slavery and thought Lincoln would abolish it)

No, they thought he'd make them give up slaves

✓ 7. Which state of the Confederate States was mentioned in this selection? (South Carolina)

South Carolina? Q yes S.C.

✓ 8. What do you think finally made the people of South Carolina vote to leave the government of the United States? (Lincoln's election)

When Lincoln got elected

✓ 9. What does secede mean? (any variation of leaving or breaking)

What the states did – break away

X 10. Did the Civil War start when the six states joined South Carolina to form the Confederate States of America? (no, any reasonable supporting evidence e.g. Confederacy formed in February, war began in April; text said war began with attack on Fort Sumter)

yes   *50%*

Discussion of Results

Rarely will an IRI record be as straightforward to interpret as is Allison's. Allison's scores on the IRI are relatively good reflections of her overall reading performance. The administration of only three reading levels of the inventory yielded fairly full information about her reading skills. There is also a consistency in her performance from reading level to reading level that is not present in the records of the two other children in this Appendix.

Based upon Allison's scores we would estimate her reading and listening levels to be

Independent: Fifth Reader Level
Instruction: Sixth Reader Level
Frustration: Seventh Reader Level
Listening Comprehension: Seventh Reader Level

As will be noted from the discussion which follows, qualitative analysis of Allison's performance on the IRI confirms the setting of the levels.

Oral reading. Allison's oral reading at fifth reader level was excellent. There were three substitutions and one word omitted at that level, but none of these miscues seriously threatens to alter the meaning of the passage. For example, in the first substitution she used *were* for *are* in the sentence "In order to learn more about how to help deaf people speak, Bell began to study how speech sounds are made." The word *are* appears after a verb (*began*) used in the past tense earlier in the sentence. It seems quite possible this substitution occurred because of a "grammatical set" Allison had for the past tense created by the verb that had come before. As noted in the test material, her oral reading was fairly fluent. While her rate of reading was not rapid, it seems likely Allison was slowing her rate of reading to achieve accuracy.

At sixth reader level, however, the nature of Allison's miscues seems more serious. There is a shift from making substitutions which are semantically close, though visually dissimilar, to the word printed in the selection (e.g. *were* for *are*) to substitutions semantically distant, though visually similar (e.g. *old* for *odd* and *stripes* for *ships*). It is important to note that Allison still seemed to be reading for meaning. She did correct her reading of *stripes* to *ships*. It seems probable Allison realized calling camels "stripes of the desert" didn't make sense so she reread and corrected the error. Allison did not reread to correct some of the less obvious shifts in meaning made as a result of miscues. For example, Allison substituted *desert* for *deserts* in the phrase "the great deserts of Asia and Africa." While in reality it is not reasonable to think of a desert spanning two large continents, it seems possible that Allison didn't make such a judgment and, therefore, didn't correct her substitution. The concepts of deserts and the continents of Asia and Africa may not have been formed fully enough to make her realize that *desert* substituted for *deserts* did not make good sense.

At seventh reader level the number of miscues and repetitions increased and seemed more disruptive to meaning. For example, she read "Here the temperatures are more moderate, neither as hot in the summer nor as cold in winter." as "Here the temperatures are more modern and newer and hot in the summer and as cold in the winter." Clearly, the meaning of the sentence is lost and thus the errors don't even fit the syntax of the sentence. It is also noteworthy that Allison had difficulty with two proper nouns, *Yangtze* and *Takla*. She needed examiner help with Yangtze and mispronounced Takla. Two diagnostic hypotheses seem reasonable based on these latter miscues. First, it seems probable that these are geographic terms Allison had not heard before. Second, it seems that when faced with a visually unfamiliar word, she is rather unsystematic in applying word analysis skills — *Takla* was not represented well phonically by Allison.

Thus, the qualitative analysis of oral reading seems in harmony with the conclusions one would draw from Allison's oral reading scores. This is not the case with all IRI performances. In terms of Allison's oral reading in context scores and the quality of her oral reading, materials at fifth reader level can be read accurately and with facility; those at sixth reader level present challenges requiring teacher guidance; and materials at seventh reader level are too difficult.

It is important to keep in mind that we have been discussing only oral reading performance. It is possible for someone to turn in a very acceptable oral reading performance at a particular reader level and yet not have the background knowledge and skills to be able to meet the comprehension demands of that level material.

Oral rereading. Allison seems to be developing the ability to scan previously read materials to locate information needed to answer a specific question posed by the examiner. She located the called for material rapidly and accurately at fifth and sixth grade levels, and her oral rereading at both levels was accurate and fluent. Though there was little room for improvement of oral reading at sight, the overall quality of the rereading seemed slightly better. In both cases, Allison was able to focus on the specific information called for; she showed no tendency to read too much of the material.

Comprehension Skills

Though the differences are small between Allison's comprehension scores based on materials she read silently compared with those she read orally, the differences are consistently better for silent reading performance at both levels of the IRI. It seems possible that Allison finds the need to read orally distracting and this detracts from her ability to focus on understanding the material. Given her general level of performance, this seems neither terribly unusual nor a serious problem.

At fifth and sixth reader levels, most of the questions Allison was not able to answer were factual recall questions. Her answers to comprehension questions generally reflected a basic understanding of the selections and the ability to remember the general and important content of these selections. Her ability to draw inferences was generally good.

At seventh reader level there is a sharp decline in Allison's understanding of the material. The concepts she brings to the selection are incompletely formed, and her ability to interpret the material is more restricted. For example, her responses suggest a basic misunderstanding of the existence of large bodies of water in China, and of the effect of such bodies of water on weather. Her performance at sixth compared with seventh reader level seemed reflective of the difference between an instructional and frustration level of performance in reading comprehension; at sixth reader level it seemed likely that, with some teacher support, Allison would succeed in mastering the content of the selections; at seventh reader level it appeared the demands were so great that both pupil and teacher would be frustrated in trying to achieve mastery of the content. Because of the serious, widespread problems Allison encountered with the comprehension of the orally read materials at seventh reader level, a parallel passage was not administered to measure silent reading skills.

Allison's performance on measures of listening comprehension was somewhat better than on comparable measures of reading. She was able to demonstrate good understanding and recall of seventh reading level material when such materials were read to her. Her answers demonstrated good understanding of the content and mastery of the skills needed to interpret this content. Similar to her performance on reading comprehension, she had difficulty with some questions that called for recall of specific facts.

The fact that her performance in listening comprehension is superior to that of reading comprehension raises the possibilities that Allison's word identification skills are not developed to the point of being fully automatic. Some attention and concentration must be diverted from comprehension processing to decoding, thus making it easier for Allison to understand materials when they are read to her compared to when she reads them herself.

At any rate, it seems safe to conclude that Allison's ability to understand and remember materials read to her is somewhat better than her ability to deal with similar materials she reads herself.

Major Conclusions about and Recommendations for Allison

Allison is a sixth grade student who appears capable of benefiting from reading instruction with sixth reader level materials. The results of the IRI are in agreement with the report received from the school she attended.

A basal, developmental approach to reading seems appropriate for Allison. No outstanding areas of weakness were noted. There were suggestions in the test results that she could profit from some guidance in systematically analyzing words visually unfamiliar to her. Wide reading, particularly at an independent level, would be useful in helping her achieve greater facility and fluency in reading. She does appear to be reading for meaning and makes an attempt to make sense of what she reads. Her vocabulary skills and background of experience need to be expanded to permit her to better understand materials she reads or materials read to her.

Case Study # 2: Jeff

Background Information

Jeff is six years and ten months old; he was given an IRI the beginning of October of second grade. Jeff had finished the first reader level book of a basal reader series in first grade, and his first grade teacher recommended he be placed in a second reader level book. His second grade teacher followed this recommendation, but Jeff experienced considerable difficulty when working in the second reader level group of fourteen children. After Jeff had been in the group for two and one-half weeks, the second grade teacher administered an IRI.

Testing Information

Because Jeff was experiencing difficulty, the teacher started with passages at primer level, dropped back to a preprimer selection, then proceeded to higher levels. Since decoding skills were the only areas of weakness at primer level the teacher administered only the oral reading phase of the IRI at preprimer. Given the strong performance in silent reading and comprehension at primer, it seemed unnecessary to test these skills at a lower level.

At second reader level, Jeff's oral reading performance was so labored testing was discontinued to avoid unnecessary frustration. The selection that normally would have been used for silent reading was used to evaluate listening comprehension. Listening skills were also evaluated at third and fourth reader levels.

The administration of an IRI to Jeff illustrated how the parts of an IRI can be selectively administered. Copies of the examiner's forms for preprimer (oral reading only), primer, first reader, and second reader (oral reading only) are reproduced. A summary sheet includes scores for various levels of the test and includes scores for measures of listening comprehension. Before reading *our* conclusions about Jeff's performance, study all these test results carefully, and try to answer the following questions:

1. What are Jeff's independent, instructional, frustration, and listening comprehension levels?
2. What are Jeff's major strengths and weaknesses in
   a. oral reading?
   b. reading comprehension?
3. What major recommendations would you make for improving Jeff's reading performance based on these results?

Jeff's Test Results

Preprimer Level: Oral Selection

49 words

Mother said, "~~Who~~ *How* will come with me?"

"I will go," said Sam.

Bob said, "I will not go. I want to/stay home. Can|I|stay home, Mother?"

Mother said, "Bob, you can stay home. You can stay home with Father. Sam and

I will go to the|store."

42"

$$49\overline{\smash{\big)}\,2.000} \quad .040$$
196
40

100
− 4
96%

Primer Level: Oral Selection

(63") 78 words

reading slow + choppy at first, then became more fluent

Bill and Ann were friends. Bill liked Ann.

Ann liked Bill. One day Ann got a new toy.

"Can I play with the toy?" asked Bill.

her

Ann did not want Bill to play with the toy. But Bill was her friend.

"You can play with the toy," said Ann. Ann looked sad.

"No, I will play with it after you do," said Bill.

"Let's play with it together," said Ann.

They had fun playing with the toy together.

.038 or 4%

$$78\overline{)3.000}$$
234
660
624

100
-4
96%

Questions for Primer Level: Oral Selection

✓1. Who were the friends in the story? (Ann and Bill)

✓2. What did Ann have? (A new toy)

✓3. Why didn't Ann want Bill to play with the toy? (it was new, she probably wanted to play with it herself, or any other justifiable response) *She didn't want him to play with it Q It was her toy and it was new*

✓4. Why did Ann say that Bill could play with the toy? (they were friends, didn't want to lose Bill's friendship, or any other justifiable response) *She liked him Q They played together*

✓5. Why did Bill say he would not play with the toy? (probably noticed Ann looked sad; any justifiable response) *Waited for both of them to play. It was her toy.*

✓6. What did they decide to do? (play with toy together)

✓7. How do you know they didn't fight over the toy when they played with it? (said they had fun playing) *They played together Q Had fun* 100%

108

Primer Level: Silent Selection

ORR

⌈One day Bill said, "Ann, I have a surprise."
"What is the surprise?" asked Ann.
"You try to guess what it is," said Bill.⌋
"Will I like it?" asked Ann.
"Yes, you will," said Bill.
"Can you read it?" asked Ann.
"No, you cannot read it," said Bill.
"Can you eat it?" asked Ann.
"Yes, you can eat it," said Bill.
"I think I know what it is," said Ann. "I think that it is a book."

Questions for Primer Level: Silent Selection

✓1. Who had a surprise? (Bill)

✓2. What did Bill want Ann to do? (guess what the surprise was)
Guess the surprise

✓3. What was one thing that Ann asked about the surprise? (Will I like it, or can you read it, or can you eat it?)

✓4. What did Ann guess the surprise was? (a book)

✓5. Do you think Ann was right? Why? (no, either you can't eat a book or Bill said you can't read it)

✓6. Think about what Bill said about the surprise. Name one thing you think the surprise might be. (any response reflecting the clue that it is something that can be eaten) *I think it's candy. I like candy.*
100%

Oral Rereading

Read the sentence which tells what Bill told Ann to do.
Starts at the beginning. Reads line by line.
Did stop appropriately — no word rec. problems —
some improvement in rhythm of oral reading.

First Reader Level: Oral Selection

$$81\overline{)5.000}$$
$$\begin{array}{r} .061 \\ 486 \\ \overline{140} \\ 81 \end{array}$$

$$\begin{array}{r} 100 \\ -6 \\ \overline{94}\% \end{array}$$

Mom and Dad were going out to have dinner. Beth and John will stay home with

ss – become

a sitter. They like to have sitters because then they can eat *out* TV dinners.

"Is Jane the sitter tonight?" asked Beth.

Beth liked Jane the best.

"No, it will not be Jane," said Mom. "Jane has too much homework to do. The

sitter is someone new, and his name is Tim."

then

Beth looked at John, and John looked at Beth. This was a big surprise.

(1'22")

Second half of selection somewhat more fluent

Questions for First Reader Level: Oral Selection

X 1. Where were Mom and Dad going? (out to dinner)

To a movie

✓ 2. How do you know Beth and John were not grown ups? (they were to have a sitter) *Jim had to baby sit them*

✓ 3. Why did Beth and John like to have sitters? (could eat TV dinners)

Liked TV dinners

X 4. Who did Beth want the sitter to be? (Jane)

I forgot her name.

X 5. How do you know Jane went to school? (had homework)

DK

✓ 6. Who would the sitter be? (Tim)

✓ 7. Why were Beth and John surprised? (any logical response that can be justified e.g. surprised because it was a new sitter, perhaps surprised because sitter was a boy) *They usually had Jane, Jim was new.*

✓ 8. In this story what does the word <u>sitter</u> mean? (someone who takes care of children) *A baby sitter ⱷ Takes care of you.*

63%

ORR

Beth and John had never had a boy for a sitter before.

"I like Jane for a sitter," said Beth. "She can pop popcorn, and she lets us watch

TV."

"I like Jane too," said John. "She reads good stories to us before we go to bed."

Soon the doorbell rang, and Tim was there. Mom and Dad left for dinner.

"Well," said Tim. "What would you two like to do now?"

"Do you know how to pop popcorn?" asked Beth.

"Sure, I do," said Tim.

Questions for First Reader Level: Silent Selection

1. What do you think would happen next in the little story you just read? (probably they would pop popcorn; any justifiable response)

   Eat popcorn Q make it

2. What was different about the sitter Beth and John were going to have? (he was a boy) ✓

3. Why did Beth like Jane for a sitter? (either she popped popcorn or she allowed them to watch TV)   *made popcorn*

4. What did John like to do before he went to bed? (listen to a story)

   Eat popcorn Q DK

5. How did the family know when Tim came to their house? (heard a doorbell) ✓

6. How do you think Beth felt at first about having Tim for a sitter? Why? (probably she didn't like it; she liked Jane or any logical response)

   She didn't like it   Q liked her old sitter

7. How do you think Beth felt about having Tim for a sitter at the end of the story? Why? (better, he said he knew how to pop popcorn)

   Liked him because he could make popcorn

8. Were Mom and Dad still home at the end of this story? How do you know? (no, said they left for dinner) *said they went*

   88%

Oral Rereading

Read the sentence which tells why John liked Jane as a sitter.

Read too much again. See section marked.

113

Second Reader Level: Oral Selection   124 words

"I can't do this. The words are too hard."

||| Midnight was Jen's horse. Jen's Uncle Joe had given the horse to her. Jen was a *(Jan's house Jan's)* *(give house Jan)* little girl, but she tried hard to help care for Midnight. When Dad brushed Mid- *(wxw lit-le)* *(tried her ✓)* night's shiny coat, Jen always helped. Jen also helped Dad put out hay for the horse to eat.

Dad said that it was important to take Midnight for a ride everyday. Jen wanted to ride the horse across the fields. Father said that Jen could not ride the horse outside the yard. Jen did not like staying in the yard. She wanted to take Mid- night for a far ride. It would be so easy for Jen to open the gate. If she opened the gate, she could take Midnight for a long ride.

discontinued

Second Reader Level: Listening Selection   122 words

One morning Jen was riding Midnight in the yard. It was a lovely spring morn- ing. The horse seemed to feel good, and Jen felt great. She began to get angry with Father for not letting her ride outside the yard.

Father was busy at a meeting in the house. He would be there for hours. All she had to do was open the gate. Then she and Midnight could ride across the open fields. She stopped the horse and got off. She walked over to the gate, but she decided not to open it. She would not break her promise to Father.

Just then Jen was surprised to see Father coming to the yard. He was bringing his friends to see Midnight.

Questions for Second Reader Level: Listening Selection

1. What time of the day was it when Jen was riding Midnight? (morning)

2. What do you think the weather was like? (any response reflecting that it was a nice spring morning) *Sunny and nice — made everyone feel good*

3. Why did Jen begin to feel angry? (wanted to ride outside yard but Father wouldn't permit it) *Couldn't go past gate with her horse*

4. Why might Jen have thought she could ride outside the yard and not get caught by Father? (he was in a meeting that was to last for hours) *Was with his friends at a meeting*

5. Was Jen going to take Midnight out of the yard? Why do you think so? (probably — she got off the horse and went to the gate) *No, promised her father*

6. What made Jen decide not to take Midnight outside the yard? (she had promised Father) *Said she promised him*

7. What do you think would have happened if Jen had opened the gate and had taken Midnight out? (seems likely Father would have found her doing it) *Would have broken her promise — Father would be angry*

8. Who was with Father? (his friends)

88%

115

Third Reader Level: Listening Selection

There had always been just four people living in the Wendell house. Now Grandma was coming to live with them. Sam and Judy didn't really know how they felt about that. They were used to living with just their parents. Would things be different now? They really liked Grandma, but she had a way of being a little bossy. They wondered if she would make them wear a hat when they went outside in the winter. Would they ever be able to walk around the house in bare feet? Grandma always seemed to worry that they would catch colds.

Judy and Sam liked to read, but they also liked to watch TV. Grandma thought it was a waste of time to watch TV. Grandma said she would always have time to read to them, and they did like to be read to. Grandma also bought them a lot of good books.

Questions for Third Reader Level: Listening Selection

✓1. What was Judy and Sam's last name? (Wendell)

✓2. How many people would soon be living in the Wendell house? (5)
   Mother, Father, Sam, Judy and Grandma = 5

✓3. Who was coming to live with them? (Grandma)

✓4. What did the children worry about wearing in the winter? (hats)

✓5. Why do you think their Grandma thought it was a bad idea to walk around in bare feet? (implied it lead to colds)
   Thought they would catch colds

✗6. Why might you think Grandma liked the children? (said she'd read to them, concern for their health, bought books for them; any of the preceding answers or other justifiable answer)
   Was coming to live with them

✓7. Name two things Judy and Sam might like to do in their spare time. (read, watch TV)

✓8. Do you think it would be a good idea for Judy and Sam's parents to buy Grandma a TV for her new room? Why? (probably not; she thought watching TV was a waste of time)
   She didn't like to watch TV.

✓9. What do you think Grandma might buy Judy and Sam for presents? Why? (books) *Hats and slippers so they wouldn't catch cold*

✗10. Name one thing Grandma did that Judy and Sam liked. (read to them)
   Came to live with them Q DK

   80%

117

Fourth Reader Level: Listening Selection   149 words

Leaves are so common in our lives that it is easy to hardly take notice of them. Yet the simple leaf is needed by all living things.

The life of a plant depends on its leaves. The leaves combine water, air, and sunlight to make food for the plant.

Animals also need leaves to live. Grass is really a lot of green leaves growing close to each other. Many animals eat grass for food so it is good there are more grass leaves than any other kind of leaf. Cows, for example, can live on a diet of grass and water.

Human beings also need leaves in order to live. Many of the vegetables we eat are leaves. The meat we eat comes from animals who are able to live and grow because they eat leaves. We need leaves to live as much as plants do.

Questions for Fourth Reader Level: Listening Selection

X1. What is this story about? What is its main idea? (all living things depend on leaves) *Leaves* Q DK

√2. Why is it so easy to not notice leaves (they are so common)
They're all over the place

X3. What three things do leaves use to make food for a plant? (water, air, and sunlight) DK

X 4. What did this article say that grass was? (lots of leaves growing together)
Green Q DK

X5. People don't usually eat grass. In what way does grass make food for people? (through animals; people eat meat from animals and animal products such as milk) *It doesn't*

√6. What animal was mentioned that can live on leaves and water? (cow)

√7. What does the article call leaves people eat? (vegetables)

43%

Summary of Jeff's IRI Scores

Reading

Level	Oral Reading in Context	% Oral Comprehension	% Silent Comprehension	% Average Comprehension
Preprimer	96	Not Administered		
Primer	96	100	100	100
First	94	63	88	76
Second				
Testing Discontinued				

Listening

Level	% Comprehension
Second	88
Third	80
Fourth	43

Interpretation of Jeff's Test Results

Reading and listening comprehension levels. Based on the test results, there is no level at which Jeff met the criteria for an independent level. Testing was begun with the primer level selection. While comprehension was excellent at primer, Jeff needed the examiner's help with two of the sixty-three words; he also substituted the word *her* for *the*. Because it seemed to the examiner that Jeff had not met the criteria for an independent level at primer, Jeff was next asked to read a preprimer selection aloud. While the overall quality of the reading was slightly better, some difficulty still existed with oral reading. Jeff needed examiner help with *stay* the first time it appeared in the selection, and he substituted *how* for *who,* although he did return to correct this.

Jeff's teacher did not ask him the comprehension questions for the orally read preprimer selection nor did she administer a selection for him to read silently at this level. His excellent performance with the primer selection strongly suggested that word identification, not comprehension, was the limiting factor in Jeff's reading. Therefore, the teacher felt nothing would be gained by checking reading comprehension at a level below one where Jeff exhibited complete understanding.

From the test results, the teacher concluded that second reader level was definitely too difficult for Jeff. At second reader level, Jeff's reading was definitely at a frustration level. He was struggling so much with oral reading, the teacher decided to discontinue the testing. Deciding to discontinue testing when the child is reading a passage is always a difficult decision to make. Allowing the child to finish the passage gives the examiner more data from which to draw conclusions; in addition, stopping the child may be perceived as a reflection of the examiner judging the performance so poor it needs to be stopped. On the other hand, a child struggling as much as Jeff was will frequently feel relieved to have the testing discontinued. This was the case with Jeff. He had little self-confidence (see some of the comments on the examiner's record forms), and once he ran into difficulty with oral reading, he seemed to be unable to apply skills he had previously demonstrated.

Jeff's teacher concluded that primer level materials would be best for instruction. Jeff's strong comprehension can be capitalized upon and his word recognition difficulties are minimal. First reader level may also seem like a reasonable possibility as an instructional level for various reasons. First, the numerical criteria for an instructional level are almost met. The word recognition in context score was 94 percent and the average comprehension score was 76 percent. Second, the purpose of reading is to obtain meaning, and when Jeff wasn't required to do oral reading, his silent comprehension was good (88 percent). In spite of these positive points, first reader level was eventually rejected as an instructional level for several reasons. There was a sharp drop in the quality of oral reading from primer to first reader level. Repetitions were made several times at first reader level, probably in an effort to gain and consolidate meaning. Pauses were more frequent and pronounced. Errors which did not fit the meaning of the sentence and passage were allowed to stand. For example, one sentence was eventually read as: "They like to have sitters become then they can out TV dinners."

Third, while the average comprehension score was acceptable in terms of numerical criteria, serious problems with word recognition were detracting from comprehension, especially for the oral reading passage. Fourth, while comprehension was good for the first reader level silent passage, the examiner noted that substantial effort appeared to go into the reading of the passage. It was read slowly, there was a request for examiner help, and there was much rereading of the passage in an effort to understand the content. Finally, because Jeff seemed so insecure about his reading ability, the teacher decided that a level where the probability of day to day success was high was appropriate for instruction.

Jeff's listening comprehension was set at third reader level. His performance on the IRI passages suggested he has the interest, word meaning knowledge, and ability to understand connected text required to deal with materials written at a level higher than his grade placement. These results lead to the conclusion that his limitations in reading are due to decoding or word identification problems rather than to limitations in language, motivation, or attention.

In summary, the levels were set as follows

Independent: Very easy to read materials
Instructional: Primer
Frustration: Second reader level
Listening Comprehension: Third reader level

Students of IRIs frequently ask one question with respect to a summary similar to the previous one: What about materials at first reader level; if they're not in-structural materials, aren't they frustration level materials? Our conclusion is that they are neither. It would be inappropriate for Jeff to be placed in first reader level materials for ongoing instruction; eventually, problems would arise. However, if a selection at first reader level were particularly important or of particular interest to Jeff, it could be used *occasionally* with teacher guidance. For example, a high level of interest could compensate for a higher than desirable level of word recognition challenge; or preintroduction, by the teacher, of much of the new vocabulary included in a particularly important piece of reading material at first reader level could make it "readable" for Jeff, who might otherwise find it overly difficult. Our position is that such compensating considerations are unlikely to allow Jeff to work at second reader level material because of the high level of difficulty he experiences.

Finally, the gap between Jeff's instructional level of primer and his frustration level of second reader level suggests that he should be able to move through instructional materials with considerable success, fairly quickly. Since first reader level was not a frustration level for Jeff, one can conclude that he already possesses some of the skills required for successfully responding to instruction at that level.

Major Strengths and Weaknesses

Oral reading. The examiner noted that Jeff's oral reading was hesitant and slow at the start, but it became more fluent in the second half of the primer passage. It may be that Jeff is hesitant and unsure of his ability to read orally and/or that he needs some time to build context for what he reads. A lack of confidence is suggested by Jeff's reluctance to make attempts at words difficult for him, especially when such words are at the beginning of the passage. He seems to prefer to wait for examiner help.

A major strength is that Jeff seems to be reading for meaning. At preprimer level he corrects an oral reading error that doesn't make sense. The only substitution he makes at primer level fits the context of the sentence and selection. At first reader level he repeats some phrases in what is probably an effort to consolidate the meaning of the passage. In one case he goes back to correct a sentence. He corrects "No, I will not be Jane." which does not fit the meaning of the selection, to "No, it will not be Jane." which is meaningful and correct. While we judge that Jeff is basically reading for meaning, it must be noted there are some substitutions which fit the graphic characteristics of the printed word he is trying to read, but which do not make sense (e.g. *out* for *eat* or *become* for *because*). Certainly, this is true at second reader level. If the demands of word recognition become excessively burdensome, many children who basically read for meaning will adopt any strategy that will allow them to do the required reading. In many cases, when children are asked to read materials at their frustration level, they are unable to use meaning context clues and are forced to overrely on graphic clues, just as Jeff did at second reader level.

Another definite strength for Jeff is that he seems to be making progress in developing the ability to recognize, on sight, "high frequency vocabulary" – those words (e.g. *the, was, to, I, go*) which occur repeatedly in the English language. Jeff tends to have more difficulty with words less likely to be constantly repeated in beginning reading materials (e.g. *stay, friends, sitter, dinner, homework, Midnight, Jen*).

Jeff has the ability to effectively divide words into syllables or to divide compound words into their base words. His treatment of *sitter* and *homework* at first reader level and even his ill fated treatment of *little* at second reader level seem to reflect some internalizing and ability to use word analysis techniques that go beyond treating individual letter sound associations. Some efficiency in word analysis seems to be developing.

Letter sound correspondences for initial consonants appear to be elements Jeff has well in hand. Even words misidentified were correctly pronounced with respect to beginning letters. In fact, Jeff almost always correctly identifies the beginning parts of words. Errors with middle and end parts of words are much more common. A listing follows of all errors or miscues made by Jeff.

Miscues Made by Jeff

Level	Word	Response	Notes
Preprimer	stay	0	corrected
	who	how	corrected
Primer	friends	0	
	liked	0	
	the	her	
First	dinner	0	
	because	become	
	it	I	corrected
	–	then	insertion
Second	Midnight	0	Examiner prompt
	Uncle	0	
	Jen's	Jan's	3 times
	horse	house	2 times
	given	give	
	little	lit-le	
	tried	tired	
	hard	her	

It is dangerous to draw too many conclusions from such a small list of deviations from what was printed in the selections Jeff read. This is particularly true since half of these deviations from print were at second reader level where the frustrating nature of the material likely prevented the application of skills Jeff could apply to materials at a more appropriate level of challenge. For example, one might be tempted to look at his substitution of *tired* for *tried* and conclude that he has difficulty with consonant blends. While it might be true that Jeff has difficulty with such elements, it is unwarranted to draw a clear conclusion from one example taken from a passage difficult for Jeff to read.

A summary of some of Jeff's major strengths and weaknesses as reflected in oral reading include:

Strengths	Weaknesses
Reads for meaning	Has little confidence in reading ability
Uses context clues	Loses meaning as word recognition difficulties increase
Recognizes high frequency vocabulary instantly	Needs to extend instant recognition vocabulary
Focuses word attack on elements beyond single letters	
Reflects beginnings of words accurately	Ignores middle and ending of difficult words

Looking at the summary, you might make two immediate observations. First, the summary doesn't address all possible skill areas; for example, what about digraphs, blends, and diphthongs? Even a full IRI won't answer all questions. Answers to additional questions are probably best derived from careful observation during instruction. Second, how is it possible for the list of strengths to be longer than the list of weaknesses for a child in second grade who is reading at primer level? While we would take the position that Jeff is certainly not reading as well as he might, we also feel it important for a teacher to know the strengths on which he can build. In Jeff's case, we see numerous strengths along with some obvious limitations.

Major recommendations. Jeff should be instructed using primer level materials. While a basal reader approach could be used to continue skill instruction, it might be profitable to use language experience activities to capitalize on his rich language skills and to provide him with opportunities to deal with a wide range of printed materials.

The extent to which Jeff has mastered and can apply knowledge of consonant blends, digraphs, and vowel sounds should be assessed through trial teaching.

Case Study #3: Carol

Background Information

Carol is an eight year old who transferred to the third grade of a new school in mid January. She had been attending a school which used what they called an eclectic approach to teaching reading—the use of library books and basal reader materials from several reading series. The report sent to Carol's new school by her former teacher indicated that Carol was reading at fourth level with 90 percent comprehension. "Carol recalls facts well, is learning to state the main ideas of selections, and tends to 'tune out' important information not related directly to plot development. With respect to word analysis, Carol can locate words in a dictionary and is working on word endings (ing, ed, es, s, and changing y to i)."

Carol's new teacher found this report somewhat confusing. First, the conclusion that this third grade student reads fourth reader level with 90 percent comprehension and recalls facts well seemed inconsistent with her "tuning out" of important information. Second, the focus on inflectional endings (s, ed) seemed unusual for someone reading at, or above, fourth reader level and for someone who already possesses basic dictionary skills. Inflectional endings tend to be taught early in most programs.

During the first few days in class, Carol's new teacher observed that she was an outgoing, verbally expressive child. In many respects, Carol seemed like a child who might be reading above her grade placement. However, an IRI seemed desirable for obtaining more diagnostic information about Carol's reading and for making a more informed judgment about instructional placement. Carol's new teacher administered IRI selections ranging from second reader level through fifth reader level as the reading portions of an IRI, and sixth and seventh reader level passages were administered to measure listening comprehension.

Summary of Carol's Scores

In addition to the IRI, Carol's teachers administered a word recognition test and an informal spelling test. All of Carol's scores were included on a Summary Sheet used at the school she was entering. Carol's scores are included on the sheet; however, only the results from the IRI are discussed here. Portions of the Summary Sheet have not been completed in order to encourage you to actively interpret the results as they are presented and to estimate levels from the IRI information.

Name _____ Case # _____ C.A. 8-1 Grade 3(?) Date 9/11/00

School _____ Examiner _____

1. Data

Level	Word Recog. Test Timed %	Word Recog. Test Untimed %	Spell. Test %	IRI Oral W.R.	IRI Oral Comp.	IRI Silent Comp.	IRI Average Comp.	IRI Listening Comp.	ORR	WPM Oral	WPM Silent
PP	100	100									
P	100	100									
1	95	100									
2	100	100	90	95	88	100	94		I	120	229
3	95	100	80	95	90	79	85		I	162	201
4	90	100	50	93	100	50	75		I	144	178
5	80	90		95	70	90	80		I	157	137
6	85	90						86			
7								70			
8											
9											

2. Estimated Levels

Independent _____ Frustration _____

Instructional _____ Listening _____

3. Recommendations

4. Summary of Specific Needs

125

Given Carol's numerical scores, what tentative conclusion would you draw about her reading and listening comprehension levels? Review the scores, and think through your response before reading on. Then compare your thoughts with the discussion in the next paragraphs.

One of the most outstanding features of the numerical summary of Carol's performance is that the oral reading word recognition scores are virtually the same from second through fifth reader levels. With most youngsters, we anticipate percentage scores will decrease as the readability levels of selections increase. Carol's comprehension scores don't show a clear pattern of becoming poorer as the readability level of the passage increases. If we attempted to establish reading and listening comprehension levels on the basis of numerical criteria only, we would be forced to conclude something like the following.

Independent level. Not established; below second reader level. While the criterion for an independent level is met by the average comprehension score at second reader level, the expected percentage score (99 percent) for accuracy of oral reading on an independent level is not met.

Instructional level. Second through fifth reader levels, and possibly higher. Carol's performance at all levels tested falls within the criteria for an instructional level. The scores for comprehension of material read orally at second and fifth reader levels are sufficient for an independent level, but the silent comprehension or average comprehension scores are not. The silent comprehension score at fourth reader level is at frustration level. However, given the overall performance, at no point does Carol meet the criteria for either an independent or a frustration level.

Frustration level. Above fifth reader level.

Listening comprehension level. Sixth and seventh reader levels, possibly higher.

Where should Carol's teacher place her for instruction? While the concept of an instructional range is a good testing concept and a good way of describing how children actually function in reading, thinking in terms of instruction anywhere from second through fifth reader level is overly broad and too general for making a decision about instructional placement.

Carol's performance is a dramatic illustration of the need to go well beyond numerical criteria when interpreting the results of an IRI. Carol's overall record on this reading measure is a rich source of information for a teacher concerned about planning an instructional program. For this reason, we will look at the results of Carol's performance at each reader level, second through fifth, and comment on the results.

Carol's teacher used a combination of retelling and questioning to assess comprehension. Therefore, after each selection, we have listed Carol's retelling of that selection. This is followed by the comprehension questions prepared in advance and used by Carol's teacher to further check comprehension. Questions preceded by an *R* are ones Carol's teacher credited, even though they weren't asked, based on information contained in the retelling.

Protocol Materials for Carol

Second Reader Level: Oral Selection

him ✓   124 words

(62")

Midnight was Jen's horse. Jen's Uncle Joe had given the horse to her. Jen was a

little girl, but she tried hard to ~~help~~ care for Midnight. When Dad brushed Mid-

                                                        away ✓

night's shiny coat, Jen always helped. Jen also helped Dad put ~~out~~ hay for the

horse to eat.

Dad said that it was important to take Midnight for a ride everyday. Jen wanted

to ride the horse/across the fields. Father said that Jen could not ride the horse

        of

outside the yard. Jen did not like staying in the yard. She wanted to take Mid-

        long

night for a ~~far~~ ride. It would be/so/easy/for Jen to open the gate. If she opened the

gate, she could take Midnight for a long ride.

$$123 \overline{)6.000} \quad \begin{array}{r} .048 \text{ or } 5\% \end{array}$$
$$\begin{array}{r} 492 \\ \hline 1,080 \\ 984 \end{array} \quad \begin{array}{r} 100 \\ -5 \\ \hline 95 \end{array}\%$$

Carol's Retelling of Second Reader Level: Oral Selection

It was about a little girl who has a horse and she wants to ride it in bigger places than the yard. She doesn't do it after all (teacher asks if Carol remembers anything else). She helped her father – like – groom Midnight.

Questions for Second Reader Level: Oral Selection and Carol's Responses

✓1. What was the name of the horse in this story? (Midnight)

✗2. Who gave the horse to Jen? (her uncle Joe)
    Her grandfather

R3. Besides Jen, who do you think usually took care of Midnight? (her father)

✓4. Name one thing Jen did to help take care of Midnight. (either helped brush coat or helped feed him)

✓5. What is hay? (food horses eat)
    It's like long grass — horses eat it

R6. What did Jen want to do? (take Midnight for a long ride)

✓7. Do you think the gate to the yard was locked? (no, story said she could open it easily) *No — she could take the horse out*

✓8. Why wouldn't Father let Jen ride where she wanted to? Why do you think so? (she was small, he probably feared for her safety; any logical, justifiable response) *Her dad was probably afraid it wasn't safe for her. He might have been afraid that she might get hurt or lost.*

88%

Second Reader Level: Silent Selection 122 words

One morning Jen was riding Midnight in the yard. It was a lovely spring morning. The horse seemed to feel good, and Jen felt great. She began to get angry *getting* with Father for not letting her ride outside the yard. | ORR

Father was busy at a meeting in the house. He would be there for hours. All she had to do was open the gate. Then she and Midnight could ride across the open fields. She stopped the horse and got off. She walked over to the gate, but she decided not to open it. She would not break her promise to Father.

Just then Jen was surprised to see Father coming to the yard. He was bringing his friends to see Midnight. *(32")*

Carol's Retelling of Second Reader Level: Silent Selection

She almost opened the gate. That morning she felt great, and the horse felt good. She didn't want to ride in the yard and wanted to ride across the open field. Her dad was with his friends in the house, but then he brought his friends out to see Midnight. She was really glad she didn't open the gate and go out riding with Midnight.

Locates easily.
Seemed to scan
for word
"angry."

Questions for Second Reader Level: Silent Selection and Carol's Responses

R1. What time of the day was it when Jen was riding Midnight? (morning)

2. What do you think the weather was like? (any response reflecting that it was a nice spring morning) *It was like spring and it felt great to ride the horse.*

3. Why did Jen begin to feel angry? (wanted to ride outside yard but Father wouldn't permit it) *She really wanted to ride that horse but her father said no.*

4. Why might Jen have thought she could ride outside the yard and not get caught by Father? (he was in a meeting that was to last for hours) *He was in the house meeting for many hours.*

5. Was Jen going to take Midnight out of the yard? Why do you think so? (probably; she got off the horse and went to the gate) *Not really she wouldn't break her promise*

6. What made Jen decide not to take Midnight outside the yard? (she had promised Father) *Didn't want to break her promise*

7. What do you think would have happened if Jen had opened the gate and had taken Midnight out? (seems likely Father would have found her doing it) *Her father would have been mad*

R8. Who was with Father? (his friends)   *100%*

Oral Rereading

Read the sentence that tells why Jen was feeling angry.

Interpretation of Carol's Performance at Second Reader Level

The quality of Carol's oral reading at second reader level was not nearly as fluent as one would expect from a third grade student, supposedly reading at least a year above grade level. There were a number of hesitations, repetitions, and substitutions in her oral reading. Nevertheless, recognition of the printed words was rapid; her overall reading rate of 120 words per minute is reasonably good for second reader level materials. It is important to note there were no words which seemed to present serious decoding problems for Carol. Words like *Midnight, brushed,* and *horse* were recognized rapidly and accurately. Other important features of Carol's overall reading performance were her drive toward meaning and her unwillingness to allow miscues to stand if they were semantically or syntactically unacceptable. For example, after reading the first sentence, "Midnight was Jen's horse." Carol began to read the second sentence as "Jen's Uncle Joe had given him...." However, she then became aware of the presence of the words "the horse to her" following the word "given" and seemed to realize the sentence "Uncle Joe had given him the horse to her" did not make sense. She repeated "had given" and on rereading, no longer inserted "him." The initial impressions gained from Carol's oral reading are that she has a good instant recognition vocabulary, she uses context and meaning clues effectively, she monitors her reading to be sure it makes sense, she corrects miscues that are semantically or syntactically inappropriate, but she is sometimes insufficiently attentive to graphophonemic clues.

When Carol was asked to read silently a second reader level passage, she did so rapidly and did not ask for help with any words. Her silent reading rate (232 words/minute) was almost twice that of her oral reading rate. A good instant recognition vocabulary and heavy use of language context clues were again suggested. This rapid reading rate for a third grader suggests that Carol may be reading to gain a general idea of the content of the selection, but she is not focusing on details. The possibility exists that she finds the materials at this level "very easy" to read.

Carol's ability to locate information within the selection she had previously read silently was rapid and efficient. She appeared to have a good memory for the material read. The quality of her oral rereading was definitely improved over her oral reading at sight. Nevertheless, she still has a tendency to underuse graphic information. The nature of the limited miscues made in oral rereading for materials previously read silently was such that virtually no distortion in meaning took place.

The content of Carol's retelling of the orally and silently read selections only partially confirms some of the diagnostic impressions gained from observation of her oral and silent reading. Her retelling of the oral selection is definitely global—lacking in detail. Initially, she doesn't even mention the name of the girl or the horse in the selection. Her first sentence is more or less "a main idea" statement of the selection; her second sentence is not based directly on the material she read. Based on this last sentence, Carol seems willing to go beyond the literal content of the selection to interpret it and to meld it with knowledge she brings to the reading selection.

Surprisingly, and in spite of her rapid reading of the silently read selection, Carol's retelling of the content of that selection is more detailed and better organized. She even recalls the specific words used to describe how Jen felt (great) and how the horse seemed to feel (good). At the end of her retelling, she again goes beyond the content of the selection and infers that Jen was "glad" she hadn't disobeyed her father.

In spite of Carol's tendency to retell the content of the selection in rather global terms, she did remember virtually all the details asked for in the comprehension questions. For example, while she did not name the girl in her retelling of the orally read selection, she remembered the name when asked. The combination of Carol's retelling of the selection and her answers to specific questions reflected good understanding and retention of the content of both second reader level selections. Carol also exhibited good language development for a third grader. She gave an excellent definition for *hay* and a well worded explanation for why Jen's father didn't want her to ride outside the yard.

Third Reader Level: Oral Selection

151 words

There had always been just four people living in the Wendell house. Now

Grandma was coming to live with them. *too* Sam and Judy didn't really know how

they felt about that. They were used to living with just their parents. Would

things be different now? They really liked Grandma, but she had a way of being a

little bossy. They wondered if/she would make them wear a hat ~~when they went~~

outside in the winter. Would they ever be able to walk around the house ~~in~~ bare

about ✓

feet? Grandma <u>seemed to always worry</u> that they would catch colds.

Judy and Sam liked to read, but they also liked to watch TV. Grandma thought

it was a waste of time to watch TV. Grandma said she would always have time to

brought

read to them, and they did like to be read to. Grandma also <u>bought</u> them a lot of

good books.

$$\left(56''\right)$$

$$151\overline{)7.000}\ \ \overset{.046}{}\ or\ 5\%$$
$$\underline{6\ 04}$$
$$960$$
$$\underline{9\ 0\ 6}$$

$$\begin{array}{r}100\\-5\\\hline 95\end{array}\%$$

Carol's Retelling of Third Reader Level: Oral Selection

It was about these kids who were used to living with just their parents. Then their Grandma was going to live with them. They weren't sure how they felt about it....Wondered if they could go out in bare feet in the summer and if they had to wear hats in the winter. Just weren't sure they would like it. They wondered if they could watch their hour or so of TV. Their Grandma also brought them good books. (teacher asked for more information) Oh, yes, their names were Sam and Jen, no Judy.

Questions for Third Reader Level: Oral Selection and Carol's Responses

✓1. What was Judy and Sam's last name? (Wendell)

I don't remember, oh yes, Wendell

✓2. How many people would soon be living in the Wendell house? (5)

5

R3. Who was coming to live with them? (Grandma)

R4. What did the children worry about wearing in the winter? (hats)

✗5. Why do you think their Grandma thought it was a bad idea to walk around in bare feet? (implied it lead to colds)

They might step on something, like glass or a pricker Q No

✓6. Why might you think Grandma liked the children? (said she'd read to them, concern for their health, bought books for them; any of the preceding answers or other justifiable answer) *Bought them books and she was willing to live with them*

R7. Name two things Judy and Sam might like to do in their spare time. (read, watch TV)

✓8. Do you think it would be a good idea for Judy and Sam's parents to buy Grandma a TV for her new room? Why? (probably not; she thought watching TV was a waste of time)

No! She hates TV

✓9. What do you think Grandma might buy Judy and Sam for presents? Why? (books) *Books — She liked books not TV*

R10. Name one thing Grandma did that Judy and Sam liked. (read to them)

90%

Third Reader Level: Silent Selection   107 words

The day came for Grandma to come live with Sam, Judy, and their parents.

Mom and Dad had painted the guest room blue, and it would now be Grandma's

room. Judy and Sam bought a nice green plant and put it on the table by the

window. Mom and Dad had bought a nice new chair for the room.

Everyone went to the airport to meet Grandma's plane. Sam saw Grandma first

ORR

and called out her name./Sam and Judy hugged her, and Mom and Dad told her

how happy they were to see her./Soon they were in the car taking Grandma to her

new home.   *Locates sentence quickly, easily.*
Oral rereading fluent + accurate

Carol's Retelling of Third Reader Level: Silent Selection

Told how their grandmother came and they were happy. They bought a green
plant for her room and painted it blue. Sam and Judy were really pleased.

(E prompt) They didn't buy her a new TV. Oh yeah, they gave her a big hug. It
didn't say where she lives but it must have been far cause she came by plane.

Questions for Third Reader Level: Silent Selection and Carol's Responses

½1. What had Mom and Dad done to get ready for Grandma's coming to live
 with them? (painted the room and bought chair)

X2. Why might you think Grandma liked the color blue? (that's the color the
 parents chose to paint her room) *Grandmothers like blue*
 Q She may have been wearing a blue dress

R3. What had Judy and Sam bought for Grandma? (a plant)

R4. Do you think Grandma was coming from pretty far away? Why? (yes, coming by airplane)

✓5. How did the family get to the airport? (car)

✓6. Who saw Grandma first? (Sam)

R7. What did Sam and Judy do after they saw Grandma? (hugged her)   79%

Oral Rereading

Read the sentences that tell something about what the children did when they saw
their grandmother.

Interpretation of Carol's Performance at Third Reader Level

While Carol's oral reading percentage scores and rate of reading are similar at
second and third reader levels, the quality of the oral reading improved at third
reader level compared with the previous level. Repetitions and hesitations are
less numerous and the fluency of reading is much better. Carol seemed less hur-
ried with the third reader selection. Though her words/minute at second and
third reader levels were similar, at second reader level she tended to read the
sentences faster, then needed to pause and repeat more frequently. There was

more "evenness" to Carol's oral reading at third reader level. Three of her seven scorable oral reading errors at third reader level were due to the omission of the phrase "when they went" in the sixth line of the selection; however, the omission resulted in virtually no loss or alteration of the meaning of the selection. The insertion of the word *too* in line two, the omission of *in* and the substitution of *brought* for *bought* in the last line are semantically and syntactically acceptable miscues. Upon rereading the last sentence in the first paragraph, she did read it without the insertion of the extra word *about*.

Two major possibilities seem to exist for explaining why Carol performed qualitatively better in oral reading at third than at second reader level. One possibility is that the second reader level section was the first administered, and Carol may have found the task somewhat unusual or anxiety provoking. Anxiety certainly can contribute to an imprecise, inefficient oral reading performance. A second possibility is that the third reader level was more challenging in terms of its decoding demands, which led Carol to slow down and pay more attention to graphophonic clues which led to a more accurate oral reading performance. Her performance at third reader level confirms that she has a good instant recognition vocabulary, uses context clues well, and monitors her oral reading performance to try to make sense of what she reads.

Carol's silent reading of the third reader level selection was similar to her performance at second reader level.

Carol's retellings of the content of the orally and silently read selections at third reader level were the reverse of what they were at second reader level. At third reader level, the content of the retelling of the oral selection was more detailed and better organized. Carol's retelling of the silent selection was brief and didn't follow the sequence of events in the passage. While the retelling of the oral reading passage was somewhat global, it reflected far more understanding of and memory for the content. The retelling of the oral selection also includes some interesting intrusions, information, and interpretations not included in the selection read. For example, the selection tells about the children wondering if they would be able to walk around the house in bare feet, but Carol's retelling has the children wondering if they will be able to go *outside* in bare feet. Likewise, the selection told about the children liking TV and about their grandmother not liking TV, but Carol's retelling reflects her inference that the children wonder if they would be able to watch TV and further specifies their "hour or so" of TV. It seems likely these intrusions are a sign of comprehension strength rather than weakness. They seem rather clear indications of Carol's active integration of information from the selection to make inferences and of her combining the content of the selection with her prior knowledge.

While blending information from the selection with prior knowledge is essential for reading comprehension, Carol sometimes overrelies on prior knowledge and fails to fully consider information presented in the selection. Her responses to the second question related to the silent selection (Why might you think

Grandma liked the color blue?) and to the fifth question related to the oral selection (Why do you think their Grandma thought it a bad idea to walk around in bare feet?) were based on her experience with grandmothers and not on information presented in the passage read.

In general, however, Carol's ability to answer questions related to the content of the selection was good. Again she remembered considerably more, as reflected in her answers, than was included in her retellings, particularly in her retelling of the silently read selection.

Fourth Reader Level: Oral Selection   149 words

Leaves are so common in our lives <u>that it</u> is easy to hardly take notice of them.

Yet the simple leaf is needed by all living things.

The life of a plant depends on ~~its~~ *it* leaves. The leaves combine water, air, and

sunlight to make food for the plant.

Animals also need leaves to live. Grass is really a lot of green leaves growing

together

close ~~to each other.~~ Many animals eat grass for food so it is good there are <u>more</u>

<u>grass leaves than any ~~other~~ kind of leaf.</u> Cows, for example, can live on a diet of

grass and water.

kinds of

Human beings also need leaves in order to live. Many of the ∧ vegetables we eat

are leaves. ~~The M~~eat we eat comes from animals who were able to live and grow

eat

because they ~~ate~~ leaves. We need leaves to live as much as plants do.   62"

$$149\overline{)10,000}$$
067 — 7%
894
1 060
10 43

$$\begin{array}{r} 100 \\ -7 \\ \hline 93\% \end{array}$$

138

Carol's Retelling of Fourth Reader Level: Oral Selection

It's about leaves and about how we need them even though we don't notice them. In fact, everything that is alive needs leaves. Grass is really lots of leaves together. Cows eat grass. People don't eat grass, but they do eat vegetables which are really leaves. If we didn't have leaves, we would all be dead. (teacher asks for more) That's all I remember.

Questions for Fourth Reader Level: Oral Selection and Carol's Responses

✓1. What is this story about? What is its main idea? (all living things depend on leaves)
   Everything needs leaves to live.

✓2. Why is it so easy to not notice leaves? (they are so common)
   They're everywhere around us.

✓3. What three things do leaves use to make food for a plant? (water, air, and sunlight)

R4. What did this article say that grass was? (lots of leaves growing together)

✓5. People don't usually eat grass. In what way does grass make food for people? (through animals; people eat meat from animals and animal products such as milk) *Take cows for instance. Cows eat lots of grass. We eat steak so we eat grass!*

R6. What animal was mentioned that can live on leaves and water? (cow)

✓7. What does the article call leaves people eat? (vegetables)   *100%*

139

Fourth Reader Level: Silent Selection   151 words

The leaves on many trees turn from green to bright colors and later fall off the tree. Not all leaves do this. The needles on pine trees and spruce trees are really the leaves on those trees. These leaves stay green the whole year long. There are many different kinds of leaves.

Leaves also can be very different from each other in size. There is a lily plant in India with leaves that grow to be six feet wide. These leaves float on water, but they are so big a child could sit in the middle of the leaf and not sink into the water. There are also leaves that are only the size of a pinpoint that live on water. There is duckweed that is so small it hardly can be seen. Often there are thousands of these tiny leaves growing together, and they seem to color the water green.

Carol's Retelling of Fourth Reader Level: Silent Selection

There is a leaf that if a child sits on it — well, it's six feet wide and if a child sits on it, it can stay floating.

Leaves are in many sizes, shapes, and colors. In fall some get brown and fall off the tree. Not all leaves do this. Some leaves are so small they can hardly be seen; the duckweed plant is like this.

(teacher asks for more) Leaves don't fall off evergreen and spruce trees.

Questions for Fourth Reader Level: Silent Selection and Carol's Responses

X 1. What did the first paragraph of this story mostly tell about? (color of leaves)

Leaves, Q DK

X 2. What did the second part of this story mostly tell about? (size of leaves)

Leaves Q DK

✓3. What did the word *needles* mean as it was used in this article? (leaves)

Like on a pine tree there are needles — like sharp leaves

✓4. Why might a spruce tree make a good tree to decorate at Christmas time? (stays green)

Lots of branches, tall Q has all its leaves

✓5. What kind of plant did this article say had the largest leaves? (lily)

Plant from India Q lily

✓6. In what kind of place do the plants with the largest leaves grow? (in water)

In India

✓7. Why might it be dangerous for a child to try to sit on the leaf of the lily plant talked about in this selection? (might sink or fall off into the water)

Could sink + drown

R 8. What was the name of the plant the article said had the smallest leaves? (duckweed)

X 9. How small did the article say the smallest leaves were? (small as a pinpoint)

very small Q DK

X 10. Where would you expect to find these smallest leaves growing? (in water)

Didn't say

Note: Answers all questions after rereading selection a second time.   60%

Oral Rereading

Find and read aloud the sentences that tell about leaves that stay green all year.

Not administered

Interpretation of Carol's Performance at Fourth Reader Level

Very few diagnostic observations can be derived from Carol's performance at fourth reader level. Though her percentage score for oral reading is slightly lower than it had been at the two previous levels (93 percent as compared with 95 percent), this difference does not seem significant and the quality of the oral reading is relatively good, comparable to what it was at third reader level. Most of the miscues are minor in nature. For example, she read the sentence "Grass is really a lot of green leaves growing close to each other." as "Grass is really a lot of green leaves growing close together.", hardly a major alteration in meaning even though the combined substitution/omission involved were counted as three errors. Likewise, the substitution of "kinds of" in line nine does virtually nothing to detract from the intended meaning of the selection and probably reflects the fact that Carol is translating print into an oral language form that reflects her own oral language development. This is more desirable than a labored, but accurate, word by word rendition of the selection.

Carol's retelling of the orally read fourth reader selection seems typical of her other retellings. She begins with a restatement of the main idea of the selection and includes some details. Her retelling of the silently read selection is less typical. Here she focuses on a fact that appeared midway through the selection. It seems likely she was very interested in a leaf large enough to hold a child. Only after talking about this interesting item does she return to give a general overview statement of the content of the selection. Her last sentence again reflects her integration of prior knowledge and content included in the selection. She talks about "evergreens" even though this term was never used in the selection.

Probably the most outstanding departure from her performance on previously read passages was her sharp drop in ability to answer questions based on the fourth reader silent selection. Since the content and concepts of the silent selection were similar to the oral selection (about which she was able to answer *all* questions), her weak performance was surprising. In an effort to better understand Carol's performance, rather than evaluating oral rereading skills, her teacher asked her to silently reread the selection after she had been asked all of the questions. After rereading the passage silently a second time, Carol was able to answer *all* the questions without hesitation. Thus, the teacher's departure from the routine IRI administration procedures yielded valuable information. The content/concepts included in that passage were not too difficult for Carol. Given an opportunity to reread and some forewarning about what she would be asked, Carol demonstrated excellent understanding and retention of the content. There is a possibility that Carol did not pay enough attention to the material during the first silent reading; a second possibility (though not substantiated by Carol's performance with other selections) is that at this point in her reading development Carol needs teacher set purposes to improve reading comprehension.

Fifth Reader Level: Oral Selection   218 words

Alexander Graham Bell was born in Scotland. His mother was a painter, and

his father taught deaf people how to speak. Bell became very interested in/his
                                                    his   *in*
father's work. He and his two brothers began to help ~~their~~ father ~~with~~ his work. In

order to learn more about how to help deaf people speak, Bell began to study

how ~~speech~~ sounds are made.

When Bell was twenty-three years old his family moved to Canada. A year

later Bell moved again and opened a school for teachers of deaf children in the

United States. At his school he studied more about how sounds were made. Then

he started to look for a way to send the sound of people's voices long distances.
Some
Other people had found ways to send noise, music, and signals long distances

over wires, but no one had been able to find a way to send *** ~~people's voices over~~
                                                      but this
~~wires. People could send~~ *** messages to each other ~~by~~ using/the telegraph, but
then
they still could not talk to each other. Bell decided he would/try to find a way to

send/voices long distances. He would spend the next few years of his life teaching

deaf people ~~and~~ trying to find a way to let people who were not in the same place,

talk to each other.   *94%*

* Note — This was one line of text on Carols copy.

                                            .064 or 6%
                                    218 / 14.000
                                       13 08
                                        920   *100*
                                        872   *-6*
                                                94%

143

Carol's Retelling of Fifth Reader Level: Oral Selection

It was about how Alexander Graham Bell taught deaf people—sort of like the way his father did and about how he was trying to invent something like the telephone. Actually that was what he invented. He was trying to find a way for people to talk to each other from long distances. People had invented the telegraph, and they could send music over wires, but no one could send voices over wires. This was what he was really trying to do. He taught in a school for the deaf and his family moved to Canada. It doesn't tell where he started the school, but I think he started the school in Canada.

Questions for Fifth Reader Level: Oral Selection and Carol's Responses

X1. Where was Alexander Graham Bell born? (Scotland)

DK

√2. From what you read, how many people do you think were in the Bell family? (5 – or 5 at least) *5*

√3. How do you think Alexander Bell became interested in helping deaf people to speak? (his father introduced him to the work)

His father probably made him interested

X4. How old was Bell when he opened a school for teachers of the deaf? (24)

DK

X5. In what country was Bell's school located? (United States)

Canada

√6. What did the article say Bell started to study to learn more about how to help deaf people talk? (how speech sounds were made)

R7. After he had been studying about how speech sounds are made, what did Bell try to learn to do? (send the sound of voices over long distances)

R8. What was invented first, the telephone or the telegraph? How do you know? (telegraph – said people could send messages with it but couldn't send the sound of voices)

√9. Name two types of sounds that could be sent over wires before peoples' voices could. (any two: noise, music, and signals)

√10. Once Bell became interested in finding a way to send voices long distances, did he spend all of his time trying to find a way? How do you know? (no, said he was teaching)

He was still a teacher   *70%*

145

Fifth Reader Level: Silent Selection

At his school for teachers of the deaf, Alexander Graham Bell began working with a friend named Tom Watson. Tom also wanted to find a way to send the sound of the human voice long distances. Bell and Watson worked for many years. Bell was a teacher during the day, and Tom worked all day in a shop. The only time they could work on their project was at night. After much work they did find a way to send the human voice over wires. When Bell was twenty-nine years old, he and Watson invented the telephone. Bell was the first one to talk on it. His first words were to Tom. He said, "Mr. Watson, come here, I want you."

Excellent, almost immediate location. Error free rereading

Bell called Tom because he needed Tom's help. Bell had spilled acid on himself, and it was burning his clothes. He was really very surprised when Tom came running in. He wasn't badly burned, but neither of them ever forgot the words Bell spoke.

After they found the way to send the human voice long distances, Bell went back to trying to help deaf people learn to speak. Bell's wife was deaf, and this may have made him even more interested in helping the deaf to speak. *91"*

Carol's Retelling of Fifth Reader Level: Silent Selection

Bell had this other guy who helped him make the telephone—Tom Watson. Bell said the first words that were said on the telephone. He said, "Mr. Watson, come here, I want you." The reason he wanted Watson was because he spilled acid on his clothes. He was surprised that Watson came even though he wasn't badly burned.

After he invented the telephone, he went back to trying to help deaf people. To make it more interesting, his wife was deaf too.

Questions for Fifth Reader Level: Silent Selection and Carol's Responses

✓1. What were the names of the two people who were talked about most in this story? (Bell and Watson)

✓2. Why might you think that neither Watson nor Bell was very rich? (both had to work) *They hadn't been in business that long. They were just trying to invent something. They probably got rich later.*

R3. What did the men in this story invent? (the telephone)

✗4. How old was Bell when he invented the telephone? (29)
25

R5. Who was the first person to talk on the telephone? (Bell)

R6. What were the first words spoken on a telephone? ("Mr. Watson, come here, I want you." accept reasonable paraphrase)

R7. Why might you think Bell was very excited when he said "Mr. Watson, come here, I want you"? (He had spilled acid, and it was burning his clothes.)

✓8. Did Bell expect the telephone to work when it did? How do you know? (no, it said he was surprised) *I saw it on an AT&T commercial. He was really surprised Q It said in the story he was surprised*

R9. What did Bell do after he invented the telephone? (returned to helping deaf people learn to speak)

R10. What might have made Bell especially interested in helping deaf people? (His wife was deaf.)
90%

Oral Rereading

Read the part of the selection that gives the first words spoken on the telephone.

Interpretation of Carol's Performance at Fifth Reader Level

Much of Carol's oral reading at fifth reader level was like that of previous levels. However, at this level she did encounter one serious problem. She missed a full line of print from the oral selection she was reading; subsequently, when she tried to make sense of what she was reading, she failed. She engaged in substitutions that were semantically and syntactically inappropriate and, for the first time in the administration of the IRI, she allowed to stand oral reading that didn't make sense. Observation of her behavior suggested she knew she was encountering difficulty, but seemed uncertain how to recover. She finally decided to finish the selection as if she never encountered the difficulty. Even at fifth reader level, it should be noted that Carol still did not encounter any word which she was unable to decode, her instant recognition vocabulary remains excellent, and she continued to correct some miscues. In fact, the oral reading score of 94 percent, including as errors the words omitted in the full line skipped, was almost the same numerical score she achieved at second reader level.

Carol was enthusiastic about reading the fifth reader level selections. A child with a profound hearing loss had spent a part of each day in Carol's class the previous year and, prior to reading the selections, Carol talked enthusiastically about this child and about Alexander Graham Bell. Her retellings, with several intrusions, again demonstrated Carol's tendency to blend her prior knowledge with the content of the selection. Her inattention to the organization and structure of the passage was apparent; she confused some of the chronology of the oral reading selection. However, the overall quality of the retelling was good. It did appear Carol was relying heavily on a rich background of experience to relate to these selections, with her inattention to details apparent in her retellings and in her difficulties answering questions about the silently read selection.

Carol's ability to respond to her teacher's oral rereading question was excellent. She seemed to be able to use a combination of memory and the graphic clues of quotation marks to almost immediately locate the first words spoken on the telephone. The oral rereading was fluent and error free. It seemed probable that Carol was familiar with this sentence from prior knowledge.

Note: At the conclusion of answering the questions based on the fifth reader level silent selection, Carol complained of being tired and expressed reluctance to continue testing. At that point she had completed four levels of oral and silent reading selections, and her teacher judged that sufficient information had been gathered to draw reasonable conclusions. Therefore, she shifted the testing from reading to listening activities. The change in activity was sufficient to allow Carol to go on willingly.

Sixth Reader Level: Listening Selection

Camels are sometimes called the ships of the desert. This is a good name for this rather odd looking creature. Without camels people could not have traveled across the great deserts of Asia and Africa nearly as early as they did.

The camel is far from being a handsome animal. It has a head that seems too small for its body and eyes which have very heavy lids and which seem to stick out from its head. Its neck is so long that it curves. Camels have thick, rough lips, and have very rough looking, shaggy fur.

Everything about the way the camel looks seems to be important for letting the camel live in the desert. The heavy eyelids protect the camel from the very bright sunlight of the desert. The eyes, which seem to stick out, let the camel see for very long distances. With its long neck the camel can reach food in trees as well as on the ground. With its thick, rough lips it can eat the hard, sometimes sharp plants that grow in the desert. The shaggy, heavy coat of the camel protects it from the heat of the desert during the day and the cold during the night.

Carol's Retelling of Sixth Reader Level: Listening Selection

Camels are called desert ships. They have rough lips and big eyelashes and eyes that sort of stick out and are yucky looking. The way a camel looks is not that great! The long neck lets it get food from trees as well as the ground. The eyes can see for long distances because they are better eyes. Their bushy fur protects them from the sun and from cold. Their rough lips let them eat hard plants in the desert. Their heads looks too small for their bodies. Their bodies are quite large.

Questions for Sixth Reader Level: Listening Selection and Carol's Responses

✓1. What did most of the article tell about? (how body of the camel is well suited to desert life) *How camels look and how they survive in the desert.*

✓2. Why are camels called ships of the desert? (they are the means that allowed people to cross deserts)

½3. On what two continents were camels used to cross deserts? (Asia and Africa)

✓4. What is unusual about a camel's face? (too small for its body) *QDK*

✓5. What does the word *protrude* mean? (stick out)

✓6. How are the camel's eyes protected from the sunlight? (thick eyelids) *Eyelids, heavy & big*

R7. What one thing about a camel might allow it to live in a cold place? (thick coat)

X 8. Why might you think camels eat lots of different things? (selection said a camel can eat from trees and the ground) *Live in the desert QDK*

✓9. Do you think camels eat plants or meat or both plants and meat? What in this article makes you think so? (everything mentioned was a plant)

✓10. Why might you think camels have very strong teeth? (mentioned that they ate hard and sharp plants) *Eat hard plants*

✓11. Why might you think that temperatures on the desert change quite a bit in a 24 hour day (hot during the day, cold at night) *Said it was hot during day & cold at night*

86%

Seventh Reader Level: Listening Selection

China has over three times as many people living in it than does the United States, but China is only slightly larger in size. Parts of China are very overcrowded because most of the people live in about one-third of that country's space. Most of the people of China are farmers, but much of the land is not suitable for farming. The richest farm land is around the Yangtze river. There are other areas of China with good soil, but in many cases they are not as productive because of insufficient rainfall or harsh long winters.

The climate in China is extreme in most places, either too hot or too cold depending on the season. This results from the fact that China is mostly surrounded by land, with no large bodies of water in it. Water heats and cools much more slowly than does land. The eastern part of China borders the Yellow Sea and the South China Sea. Here the temperatures are more moderate, neither as hot in the summer nor as cold in winter.

China contains large land areas where people cannot live. Much of the Northern border of China is desert, and the great Takla Maken Desert in the west is so dry and so large that few people, even in modern times, have ever crossed it.

Carol's Retelling of Seventh Reader Level: Listening Selection

There are three times more people in China than the U.S. The best soil part is by the Yangtze River. Other places have good soil but it is too hot or too cold. China has a desert that is so big and so hot that few people have crossed it.

Questions for Seventh Reader Level: Listening Selection and Carol's Responses

X 1. How does the size of China compare with the size of the United States? (China is slightly larger)

Same size

✓ 2. What do most Chinese people do for a living? (farm)

✓ 3. Why are parts of China especially overcrowded? (most of the people live in a third of the country) *Most of the people live in just certain parts, like where they can farm and where it's not desert.*

✓ 4. Why might you expect to find many people living around the Yangtze River? (richest farm land there)

Good for farming there

✓ 5. Why are some parts of China which have rich soil not good for farming? (long winters, insufficient rainfall) *Some parts are too hot or cold Q Some parts don't have enough water*

✓ 6. Why might you think that travel by boat would not be an important form of transportation for traveling in China? (no large bodies of water)

X 7. How do large bodies of water affect the climate of a country? (make temperatures more moderate) *Make it wet or dry Q DK*

X 8. What does moderate mean? (not extreme; in this article, neither too hot nor too cold) *I don't remember. Note: When given the passage and asked to see if she could figure out the meaning of moderate she said "more reasonable."*

✓ 9. What two seas border the eastern part of China? (Yellow Sea and South China Sea)

✓ 10. What kind of land is found in the north and west of China? (desert) *70%*

152

Interpretation of Carol's Performance in Listening Comprehension

Carol's above average background of experience and language skills is clearly reflected in her retelling of the sixth reader level passage read to her. Her discussion with the teacher prior to reading the selection suggested that she didn't know much about camels, but her interest in the topic was high. Her retelling was excellent, suggesting that she attended well to the content and to the details. Carol's abilities to answer questions based on the content of the selection and to deal with details at both sixth and seventh reader levels were good. Her response to main idea questions at the sixth reader level suggested some difficulty integrating information to form a main idea statement not given in the paragraphs read. Her first difficulty at seventh reader level came when she was unable to define the word *moderate* when first asked. Interestingly, Carol was able to arrive at an acceptable definition from context clues when her teacher directed her to read the selection to herself and try to figure out what *moderate* meant. Carol concluded that moderate meant *more reasonable,* a definition that fits the context of the selection.

Overall Conclusions Regarding Carol's Performance

The analysis just concluded is reported in far more detail than would be expected of most teachers of reading or reading specialists. In looking at Carol's performance at each reading level, the analysis does not present a sufficient overall picture. Therefore, it seems appropriate to return to some of the global questions addressed for the other two cases reviewed.

What are Carol's reading and listening levels? Now that the qualitative aspects of her performance have been considered, are they different from the levels that would be set based only on scores? What are Carol's major strengths and weaknesses in reading? Consider these questions and your interpretations before reading ours. Keep in mind that this is an eight year old child who is in the middle of third grade.

Reading Levels

Carol's independent level is probably best viewed as a range of second to third grade. Her oral reading scores at both levels fall below the criterion of 99 percent accuracy, but qualitatively the miscues were minor and did little, if anything, to detract from meaning. Her average comprehension score for third reader level falls just short of meeting the criteria for an independent level; however, her limitations in comprehension do not seem very serious. Her major problem with the third reader silent selection was that she tended to overrely on background information and to pay insufficient attention to details. She certainly seems to possess the decoding and comprehension skills to deal with language, concept, and skill demands at third reader level.

Carol's instructional level seems better addressed as a range of fourth to fifth reader level materials. One might object that this may be too low an estimate since Carol's reading was not tested with sixth reader level materials. Realistically, however, the content of materials at sixth reader level and beyond is probably not geared to the interests and experiences of an eight year old in the middle of third grade. In addition, there was enough inconsistency in oral reading and in comprehension to suggest that instruction at fourth and fifth reader levels would be profitable for Carol.

A clear frustration level in reading was not established for Carol. It is probably best to think of it as simply being "above fifth reader level."

The results of the listening comprehension evaluation place Carol's level at sixth, though she almost meets the criterion at seventh reader level. The quality of her retelling at seventh was weak and, again, it seems likely many materials at that level would be geared to interests and experience beyond that of a child Carol's age.

Strengths and weaknesses. Clearly, Carol has above average language and cognitive skills. Based on these, one would expect her to be reading above grade level. She is. She shows the skill of applying her prior knowledge in order to understand and interpret material. At times she overrelies on background knowledge and pays insufficient attention to text information.

Generally, Carol's reading comprehension skills are very strong. She follows sequence, interprets cause and effect, focuses on main ideas, and actively makes inferences as she reads. She sometimes forgets details. Based upon observation of her reading behavior, a minor problem exists in attending to or remembering details; if given the opportunity to reread in order to answer questions, she seems capable of extracting the needed information.

Carol has many strengths in word identification and oral reading. She monitors what she reads to be sure it makes sense, she generally corrects errors, and she reads in meaningful phrases. She appears to have good instant recognition vocabulary and analysis skills. She tends to use meaning clues more than graphophonic clues when reading in context. Most of the miscues she makes are minor and do not interfere with meaning; however, when reading carefully with content material (e.g. math problems, directions for a science experiment) she may need to pay more attention to graphic information.